SECOND
ROYAL GLOUCESTERSHIRE
HUSSARS

Frontispiece

SIDI BISHR

SECOND ROYAL GLOUCESTERSHIRE HUSSARS

Libya—Egypt 1941—1942

by
MAJOR STUART PITMAN

WITH A FOREWORD BY
THE DUKE OF BEAUFORT
K.G., P.C., G.C.V.O., Hon. Col.

"Quit ye like men"

The Naval & Military Press Ltd

Published by

The Naval & Military Press Ltd
Unit 10 Ridgewood Industrial Park,
Uckfield, East Sussex,
TN22 5QE England

Tel: +44 (0) 1825 749494
Fax: +44 (0) 1825 765701

www.naval-military-press.com
www.military-genealogy.com
www.militarymaproom.com

In reprinting in facsimile from the original, any imperfections are inevitably reproduced and the quality may fall short of modern type and cartographic standards.

TO THOSE WHO SERVED
AND
THOSE WHO SERVED AND DIED

FOREWORD

This book has been written so that the relations and friends of the officers and men of the 2nd Royal Gloucestershire Hussars, the officers and men themselves and the people of Gloucestershire can read of the battles fought by the Regiment in the Western Desert during the great advance of 1941 and the desperate campaign of 1942, which culminated in the final holding up of the enemy at El Alamein.

It must be borne in mind that in those early days the Regiment was far away, the Press could give but the barest general news and there was no home leave, so that Gloucestershire could not know what deeds the Regiment was performing. Therefore this will be the first account for many, and a reminder for some, of the Regiment's experiences during its time abroad. As I think is known, 2 R.G.H., having made a name second to none, was disbanded early in 1943 through inescapable circumstances—an end as untimely as it was unacknowledged. And this made it necessary for members of the Regiment to go fighting with other units, never an easy undertaking, for there is no place like " home." Nor could they achieve that victorious home-coming that fell to others, an honour that, on their record, would have been fully deserved.

At no time was their task easy. Just before the war 2 R.G.H. was formed and was given tanks instead of armoured cars in which a great many of its original members had been trained: then they had little equipment and were pre-occupied with a possible

FOREWORD

invasion. Yet they with their Brigade, all Yeomanry, went to the Middle East before many others. And this was due not only to those who went, but those who had kept the spirit and the training alive between the wars; to those who had helped to found 2 R.G.H. in its early days; and to those members of the Cavalry and Royal Tank Regiment who were posted to the Regiment and who, in spite of other loyalties, became possessed of the Yeoman spirit.

The Western Desert campaigns, fought by a few, have passed and perhaps been forgotten; but they allowed the many to prepare for the final phase, and without them that phase might never have happened. Those campaigns were fought amidst dangers and difficulties: our troops were as often as not out-numbered, out-armoured and out-gunned—indeed frequently they used American tanks considered obsolete some years before. At times rations were very short and water desperately low; it was cold in winter and intensely hot in summer; and there could be no relaxation or comfort when not in action as the Desert forbade it, and only the end of a campaign permitted leave in the Delta.

But during its year of fighting the Regiment, sharing in the triumphs and disasters of the Eighth Army, took its part in the great five-hundred mile advance to the western confines of Cyrenaica, the valiant failure at Knightsbridge, the retreat to El Alamein, and the final stopping of the Afrika Corps there at the battle of Alam el Halfa. The casualty lists—ever a sign of a Regiment's courage—and indeed the awards, vouch for the Gloucestershire Yeomanry's

FOREWORD

record. As their Honorary Colonel I commend this book as an account of the deeds that made that record and as a tribute to those who fell and those who served.

Beaufort.
Hon. Colonel
2 R.G.H.

BADMINTON
GLOS.

PREFACE

THIS book was written in manuscript in 1945. It was originally suggested that I should write it at a meeting of the R.G.H. Association in July of that year. Could I, they said, complete it by Christmas? I said that I could, and indeed the longhand version, in ink, was finished on December 23rd and was typed in double quick time by S.Q.M.S. Bywater. Since then, however, slow time has been the order. The necessary paraphernalia for printing a book has been hard to come by for many years and is even more scarce now that peace is here, and R.G.H. has, therefore, had to wait in the queue and has only, at last, come to the surface. Nevertheless I apologise to the Association for the long delay.

This history, covering a year, the only year of fighting allowed us by the god Mars, has been compiled from three sources—accounts by members of the Regiment, the War Diary and what I could remember of events myself. Members of the Regiment, generally, were shy and only a few of the many could recollect anything; the War Diary, I found, had a habit of knocking off work and putting its feet up at vital moments, but I have tried to keep the facts that have come from my own head as accurate as possible.

The maps are taken from those used by the Regimental Navigator, and his tracings of routes have been copied: the routes in the Tobruch map, are I fear, somewhat muddling, but a larger map was ruled out by the cost. They are not, however, anything like the muddle experienced at the time. The spelling

PREFACE

of place names in the text is also from the same maps. The photographs are from negatives most kindly lent by Captain G. G. Boyd and the medical officer, Dr. Waters. I apologise for keeping them so long.

I should like to thank those who sent news of their experiences and particularly those captured who enabled me to write something of what happened on the "other side." Especially I received invaluable help from Major Trevor's diary which he kept from the day of our landing till our first reformation at point 172 on December 1st, 1941; from Major Elder Jones, who wrote at length on the same period and who included a personal account of the battle of Bir el Gubi; from S.S.M. Lee, who told me of his parties' experiences at Halfaya. Later, in 1942, Tpr. V. Bridle recounts one of the more desperate battles—the battle at Bir el Harmat; Major Taylor tells of H Sqn, tout seul, in the desert during the retreat from Knightsbridge; Lt.-Col. Lloyd, D.S.O., writes of G Sqn. exploits while the Alamein Line was forming, consolidating, and repelling Rommel's final attack. To these particularly the book owes its piquancy.

Casualties were the most difficult problem. Our own lists were not, for one reason or another, accurate. They have been made out, however, from these Regimental Lists, from 2nd Echelon, Middle East, Orders, and from War Office Records. It was Lt.-Col. Lloyd who bearded War Office Records and who spent many tiring hours checking, and it is due to him that I have been able to include casualties and awards at all. If I have omitted any or included some in the wrong category, I apologise sincerely: no stone was left unturned.

PREFACE

The first proofs were read by the Padre, Rev. W. Llewellyn, and Lt.-Col. Lloyd, and subsequent proofs by Lt.-Col. Lloyd. I have received from him endless assistance and advice throughout, and it is largely due to him that the book does not contain innumerable errors and mistakes.

Finally, I thank S.Q.M.S. Bywater for his swift and accurate typing of the manuscript, done entirely in his spare time, and the Saint Catherine Press whose patience and perseverance have overcome difficulties that could not be foreseen and whose advent was not suspected by those whose deeds make this story.

S. P.

Eastcourt
Malmesbury
December 1948

CONTENTS

	PAGE
FOREWORD	VII–IX
PREFACE	XI–XIII
INTRODUCTION	XVII–XIX
CAMPAIGNS	1–85
ROLL OF HONOUR	86–89
AWARDS	90
INDEX	91–96

LIST OF ILLUSTRATIONS

Sidi Bishr . . . . *Frontispiece*

facing page

Crusader's Shadow Camouflaged from Air Observation	
Transporting a Crusader	7
German 88 mm Gun. Bir el Gubi	
Picking up R.G.H. Casualties at Bir el Gubi . .	13
A Brew-up	
Prisoners of War. Sidi Rezegh . . .	22
German Mark IV Knocked Out at Sidi Rezegh	
Crusader Knocked Out at Sidi Rezegh . .	26
De-Sanding	
El Amiriya—Mersa Matruh Express . .	35
Sunday Before Christmas Day, 1941	
Commanding Officer's Honey near El Mechili	42
Honeys near Agedabia	
Squadron Leader's Conference near Saunnu .	46
Fort Capuzzo, 1942	
B Echelon Moving Up Along the Coast Road .	53
Salum and the Escarpment	
Salum from Half-way Up the Escarpment . .	58
Grant Tank near Knightsbridge	
Desert Dust	65
Captain M. G. Ling, M.C.,	
Major W. A. B. Trevor, D.S.O.,	
Lieutenant-Colonel N. A. Birley, D.S.O.	
Major Reinhold	71
The Prime Minister Inspecting R.G.H.	
R.S.M. Lee	80
General Morshead with G Squadron	
Tobruch Cemetery	82

LIST OF MAPS

at end

Egypt and Libya
Tobruch. November–December, 1941, May–June, 1942
El Mechili. December, 1941
Agedabia. December, 1941–January, 1942
El Alamein. July–August–September, 1942

INTRODUCTION

As the pages that follow tell the day-to-day story of 2 R.G.H. during a short period of the war, it will be helpful to give, briefly, a framework in which to fit that story. Few people, other than those who were with the Regiment, knew much about its doings as censorship forbade telling even the most elementary news, and the Press were allowed to give only the list of regiments that took part in a campaign, and that when the campaign was over. Even then the names were tucked away in some obscure corner and were often inaccurate. It was not till the arrival of Field-Marshal (then Lieutenant-General) Montgomery that the immense moral value, both to the men fighting and to their people at home, of reporting the deeds of different formations was realised. It was not till he commanded Eighth Army that the letters M.E.F. ceased to mean "Men England Forget," not because England wanted to forget them, but because military censorship refused to give her any reason to remember them.

Just before the war R.G.H. was divided into two, and 2 R.G.H. was put into 22nd Armoured Brigade with 3rd and 4th County of London Yeomanry. The Brigade was commanded by Brigadier Scott-Cockburn, and the Regiments by Lieutenant-Colonel Jack Miller, O.B.E. (later by Lieutenant-Colonel Birley), Lieutentant-Colonel Jago (3rd C.L.Y.), and Lieutenant-Colonel Carr (4th C.L.Y.). As a team for training men, they were most successful, and by the time the Brigade went overseas in August, 1941, it was about as well trained as it could be without having had battle experience. It took its own tanks with it, and they were the Mk. VI Cruiser, or Crusader, the very latest cavalry tank. A few had been in action in the Desert, but this was the first Brigade to be equipped with them, and great hopes were placed in their speed and fire power. It left England ahead of 2nd Armoured Brigade, who with itself comprised

xvii

INTRODUCTION

1st Armoured Division, as it was only possible to get one Brigade out in time for the 1941 winter offensive, and it travelled in a small convoy, reaching Suez in eight weeks.

When it arrived in the line it went to 7th Armoured Division, the Desert Rats, as an additional Brigade, the others being 4th Armoured Brigade (8th Hussars, 3rd and 5th Royal Tank Regiments), and 7th Armoured Brigade (7th Hussars, 2nd and 6th Royal Tank Regiments), the whole being commanded by Major-General Gott; 7th Armoured Division was in 30th Corps under Lieutenant-General Norrie. The Division remained in this form, though getting smaller and smaller, till December 1st, when the Armour was reorganised, and 7th and 8th Hussars, 2nd and 6th Royal Tank Regiments returned to the Delta. 2 R.G.H., being the senior Regiment in its Brigade, went, equipped with Honey Tanks, to 4th Armoured Brigade, who were reforming in the line, in place of 8th Hussars. It remained with it till just before Christmas, when it returned to 22nd Armoured Brigade who came up to relieve 4th Armoured Brigade. 4th Armoured Brigade was commanded by Brigadier Gatehouse, an experienced Desert soldier, who inspired us all with great confidence and always had the measure of the Germans. 22nd Armoured Brigade remained in action till the limit of Eighth Army's advance and were relieved early in January by 2nd Armoured Brigade, its opposite number in 1st Armoured Division, who had by then come out from England.

After reforming and refitting with Crusaders and Grants in the Delta, the Brigade, commanded by Brigadier Carr, joined 2nd Armoured Brigade (Queen's Bays, 9th Lancers, and 10th Hussars) in the line in May, thus completing 1st Armoured Division, and it was still in 30th Corps. The Division was under Major-General Lumsden, a great commander of men and respected by them for his energy and courage. He believed in leading them from in front, unlike the Duke of Plaza Toro, and was invariably to be

INTRODUCTION

found as close to his leading tanks as possible. When 2 R.G.H. was withdrawn to Tobruch after the battle at Bir Aslagh, having lost the Colonel, 2nd in Command, and Adjutant, it became a continual struggle to prevent the Regiment being used as reinforcements and thereby broken up. Squadrons went to various formations for varying periods of time, and the Regiment never again appeared as a whole in the line. But there was no day when one or more squadrons were not in action, and all three fighting squadrons took part in repelling Rommel's attack at El Alamein from August 31st to September 3rd.[1] After this it was confidently expected that, in company with most of Eighth Army, it would be re-equipped in the forward area, but orders were suddenly changed and it returned to the Delta to await tanks there. Consequently it was not ready for the final battle of El Alamein and when, shortly after it, reinforcements were needed, not even the efforts of powerful allies could save it from being disbanded.

But let it not be thought that Gloucestershire Hussars saw no more fighting. F, G, and H˙ Squadrons went to 4th Hussars, Royal Wiltshire Yeomanry, and 8th Hussars respectively, while H.Q. Squadron and individuals went to other regiments, and a good number to our friends, the 5th Royal Tank Regiment and to 3rd Hussars. Many N.C.O.'s took commissions. Major-General Norman, commanding the Royal Armoured Corps in the Middle East, who interviewed them, said: "They are just the sort of fellows we have been crying out for. Why have they not taken commissions before?" But Gloucestershire Yeomen preferred to be Gloucestershire Yeomen. Members of the Regiment fought in North Africa, Sicily, Italy, France, and Germany and made a name for themselves on all those fronts. Again there were discomforts, dangers, casualties, and again there were awards. But whatever badge they wore, at heart they were still Gloucestershire Hussars.

[1] Later known as the Battle of ALAM EL HALFA.

2nd ROYAL GLOUCESTERSHIRE HUSSARS

LIBYA 1941–42

"THE officers and men of the *Strathmore* wish the 2nd R.G.H. every success and a speedy return home." With this message from H.M.T. *Strathmore*, that had taken us from the Clyde to Port Suez, the Regiment, under the command of Lieutenant-Colonel Charles Birley, landed in Egypt, the only theatre of war where British troops were fighting, on October 1st, 1941. It was met by the Colonel, who had flown on ahead from South Africa, and General Willoughby Norrie, Commander 1st Armoured Division. He doubtless had military reasons for being there—his other Brigade was still in England—but the R.G.H. felt that as a Gloucestershire man he had come to meet the Gloucestershire Yeomanry. While the troops had a meal provided by the N.A.A.F.I., natives in garments resembling night shirts assisted in carrying hand-baggage to the train. There was a great deal of shouting and noise and considerable risk that the luggage would not be seen again, for the Egyptian "fella" is an accomplished thief. The quays were littered with military equipment, some for the offensive about to begin, some from the offensive of the year before. There were Honey tanks, a tank we had sampled at Warminster and thankfully left behind. "Have they got those bloody things here?" a critic asked. We did not think that in a few weeks we should thank God and President Roosevelt for Honeys, for a tank designed in 1929 is better than no tank at all. The journey through the night to our destination, El Amiriya, some miles west of Alexandria, through the dim-out which served as black-out in Egypt, was uneventful, slow, dusty, and cold; cold to us in

2ND ROYAL GLOUCESTERSHIRE HUSSARS

tropical kit after the heat of the blacked-out ship, and cold to us who had not really believed that Egypt was ever cold. We sampled the all-pervading smell, experienced everywhere in these parts and described by Second-Lieutenant Ades[1]: "It is the Egyptian smell, a word of four letters, you will get used to it." A baggage party was left behind and another party went to unload the tanks. Delay was caused by the fact that there was only one crane in Egypt capable of unloading Crusader tanks, and it was somewhere else. Trouble was also caused by unfriendly natives purposely dropping packing cases, so that the unloading took longer than had been expected.

At 6 a.m. in the morning we arrived at El Amiriya station, and went in lorries to our camp site at Ikingi, five miles away. There we found our tents neatly folded and stacked in the sand, and also, to our surprise, permanent cook-houses and water. We set about putting up the tents, a pattern we had never seen before, and were forthwith enveloped in a sand-storm. Working against the driving sand, which forced itself into every crevice of one's clothes, body, and kit, coupled with the hot wind that makes one bad-tempered and bloody-minded, was most trying. Rations, till the Quartermaster managed to get some, were non-existent, there was little fuel for the cooks struggling to keep the sand out of the cook-houses, and it was a sunburnt, sunblasted, and exhausted regiment that hammered in the last of the very few tent pegs. We were under strict instructions from the Quartermaster not to acquire extra tentage and equipment, but this went against regimental custom, and he visited each squadron later and asked if they were comfortable and had more than they needed.

While waiting for the tanks to arrive, we trained in navigation with prismatic and sun compass, both easier

---

[1] 2nd Lieutenant Ades's father, who lived near Alexandria, was most kind to the Regiment while it was stationed at AMIRIYA, and later at SIDI BISHR. He supplied it with great quantities of fruit as well as keeping open house for the officers.

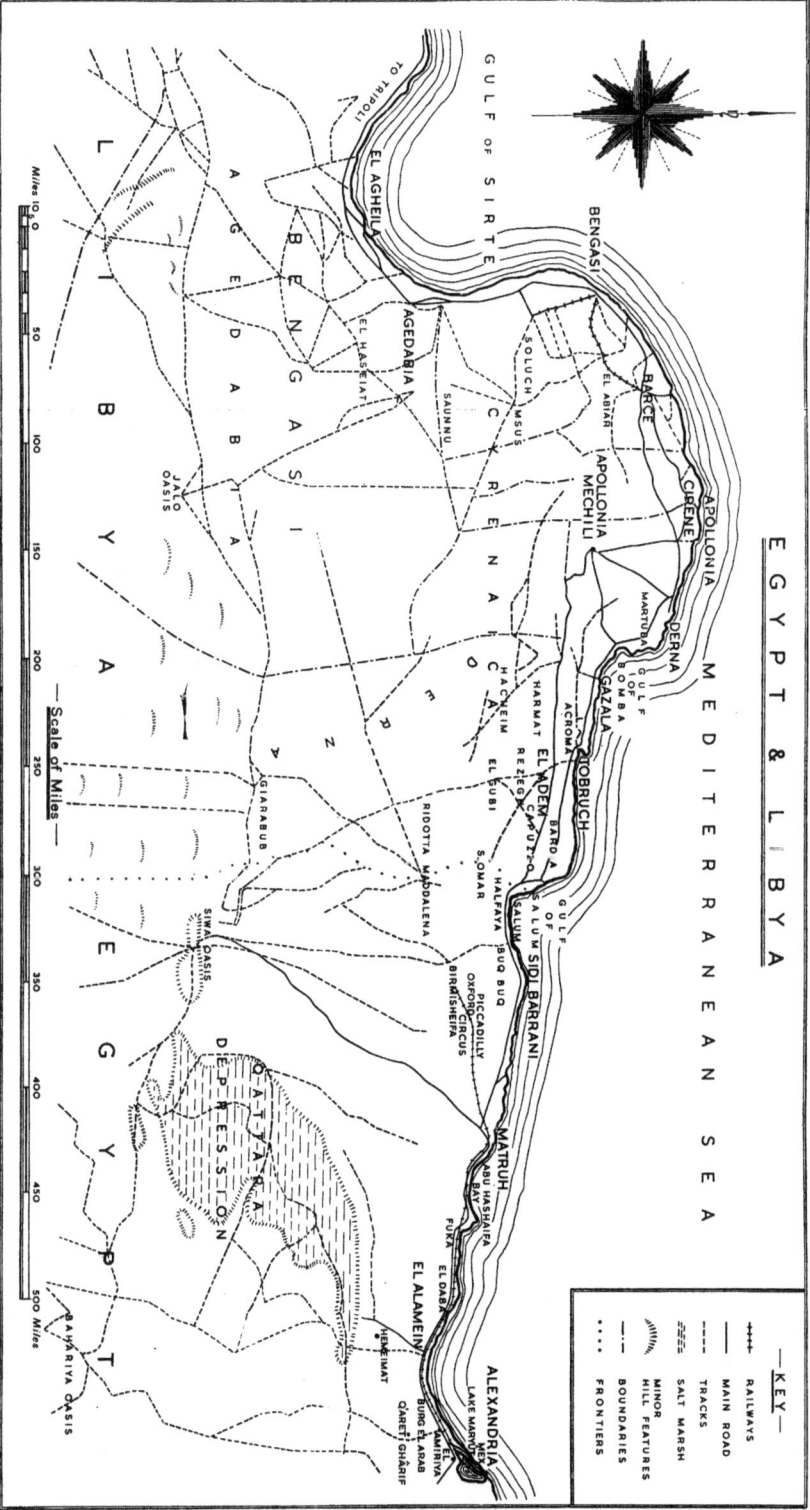

INSPECTION BY GENERAL AUCHINLECK

than was expected. It was not difficult to make an accurate landfall except when a desert fox was viewed and an attempt made to get within pistol shot, though no fox was ever seriously inconvenienced. We discovered that the desert was completely flat with hard sand but small soft patches, largely covered with camel scrub and entirely covered with small stones. Later, much farther west, we found, in addition, long, very gentle slopes and sometimes boulders that reduced a tank to walking pace. We also tried, under orders, to reduce our consumption of water so as to be ready for the small ration allowed in the forward area, but the presence of water laid on was a great temptation and it was still very hot. We found, too, that we should be on a regimental wireless net and practice was needed to prevent "Bolo," "Charlie," and "Dana" addressing their respective control stations at the same time.

The tanks, which had been to Ordnance workshops in Alexandria, then began to arrive. Various modifications had been effected, none of which had made the engines any more reliable, sandshields had been fitted, and they had been painted buff. Furthermore, the Besas had been adjusted to prevent their overheating, and also, apparently, to prevent them firing more than one shot before stopping.

Our spare time, and there was not very much, was spent bathing, which meant a walk of five miles across a salt marsh to the sea, and going into Alexandria when permitted, for baths, dinner, and whatever gaiety one felt rash enough to undertake. It was a city of plenty and, in those days, not too high prices, a city we were later to know well.

After three weeks, when all the tanks had arrived, tanks with no tools or spares and only the correct number of track pins, and with a brand new echelon, we set off into the desert to QA'RET GHÂRIF, twenty-five miles away, for Brigade training, and acclimatisation and gunnery. We had been inspected by General Auchinleck, and we took a liking to him. The "Auk," in his turn, showed no

2ND ROYAL GLOUCESTERSHIRE HUSSARS

dissatisfaction, which, from him, was enough. As the Regiment moved out, Lord Apsley, D.S.O., M.C., a Gloucestershire Hussar of thirty years standing, landed in his aeroplane to see us off.

Our march to Qa'ret Ghârif was our first effort at long distance navigation as a regiment and our first attempt on a regimental net, and both were very successful. We now lived in open leaguer, a formation always employed in the day-time, but at night only when some way from the enemy. All vehicles were two hundred yards apart, and in the dark it was easy to get lost walking from one tank to another, one or two sentries indeed finding themselves some miles away when daylight broke. Camouflage was strictly enforced and no lights of any kind were allowed at night. Crews lived by their vehicles and learned the art of "brewing up" with a petrol can filled with petrol and sand. Scorpions were a particular nuisance. There were a lot of stones, and under them they thrived. It was thought that officers in camp beds were fairly safe, but Trooper Price, packing Captain White's bed, received a bite on the index finger from his master's sleeping companion. The health of the troops was very good, thanks to the efforts of Captain Waters, the Medical Officer. He had dinned into everybody's head cleanliness and organised sanitation and the necessity for dressing and covering any scratch or cut. Consequently little but "Gippy Tummy" bothered us. We fired all our guns, and found that the alteration made to the Besas was not so dastardly as was at first thought. With practice ammunition, one shot was about the maximum. With operational ammunition, which was not, repeat not, to be used, a belt went off without a hitch. But then it was found that the practice ammunition had been made by the French during their forty-hour week Utopia. Then we set out on a Brigade exercise.

The scheme was based on what we were going to do when the attack started; we seized a piece of ground vital to

GAINING EXPERIENCE OF THE DESERT

the enemy so as to force him to attack us on it. It may have been a successful exercise from the authorities' point of view, but to many it was muddling and difficult to follow. Nevertheless, we gained experience of the desert, of close leaguering at night, of "brewing up" quickly and of spotting vehicles in the mirage which made them look fifty feet high. We got practice in filling up and repairing vehicles in the dark without lights; we sorted out supply problems, and we learned to put up with the glare from the sand and great heat—it was the hottest autumn for fifty years—and to manage on very little water. It was our first experience of thirst and not having enough water to quench it. During the heat of the day it was trying, but the cool nights eased it, and it was practice for later on when we had even less. It was decided to leave the front gunner out of action and to use his turret for stowing kit, ammunition, and supplies. It caused great disappointment to those who were to stay behind, but made it much more comfortable for the others, and, in fact, the front Besa was never required in battle. We were lent, during this time, some officers of the 7th Hussars as advisers and observers, and they were a great help in restoring our sense of balance. "It always looks like a muddle, it often is," said one of them, "but the actual business of fighting is easy enough. You go in, you come out, you go in again, and you keep on doing it till they break or you are dead. You chaps will do that O.K."

Through this strange and sometimes irritating life the Yeomanry spirit held. Routine duties were performed without orders being necessary. When they were given, the old formula, "I'd like you to . . .," "Will you please . . .," "Be a good chap and go . . .," persisted. Everybody made themselves as comfortable as they could. Major Mylne's canteen service was as good as the circumstances permitted. Eighth Army customs were adopted. We wore what we liked, from canvas shoes and shorts to change clothes. Captain White carried a deck chair on his tank for greater comfort during halts. The battle of the hat was finally decided. More Army Council Instructions were issued on hats, officers', than on most subjects. Berets were considered the correct Cavalry wear, but the Yeoman officer saw no reason why the Army Council should interfere with his regimental custom, and his service cap and blue-and-buff side hat. Now any hat was *de rigueur*; some officers affected a foreign legion ensemble with a sun flap over their necks; Lieutenant Snell sported a green pork-pie while navigating, and Lieutenant Pitman favoured a tweed cap.

After just under three weeks we returned to El Amiriya, entrained the same evening, and headed for Mersa Matruh. The journey was quiet and pleasant, and we had time to reflect that we had finished at last with training and exercises and never apparently getting anywhere, that we were heading for the front and that it had taken us two years to get there. At midnight we arrived sixty-nine miles west of Matruh and took the tanks off the train. One got stuck, and it was necessary to split the train and build a ramp of sleepers to get off the rest. Then we close leaguered till first light, when we had breakfast and put on camouflage hoods. These consisted of a framework covered with hessian, and were made to resemble the hood of a lorry. They were uncomfortable to travel under, restricting vision, and made keeping formation difficult. We set off by squadrons via "Piccadilly" and "Oxford Circus" to QA'RET AZZA, seventy-six miles south-west of Mersa Matruh and twenty-five miles east of Ridotta Maddalena, an Italian post on the frontier wire. The Echelon had come along the coast road and then across the desert, staging at DABA, GARAWLA, and MINQAR MILIHA, and by that evening the Regiment, forty-three officers, five hundred and eighty-five men, fifty-two tanks, ten scout cars, and one hundred and twelve wheeled vehicles, came into position in the line.

* * *

CRUSADER'S SHADOW CAMOUFLAGED
FROM AIR OBSERVATION

TRANSPORTING A CRUSADER

FINAL ORDERS GIVEN OUT

We settled down in open formation, not moving, to prevent making track marks and paying great attention to camouflage, moving the nets round with the sun in an attempt to deceive a reconnaissance plane which came over every morning. The tank crews spent the time on maintenance and eating their emergency rations, since the supply system had failed, while the echelon had a worrying few days trying to get rations for the tanks and their reserve supplies of petrol, ammunition, rations, and water on board. On the afternoon of November 16th news came through, which it was said was known some time before in Cairo bars, that operations were to start on the 18th, and final preparations were begun. Maintenance on the tanks was completed, guns were cleaned, ammunition was checked, and kit and provisions were carefully stowed. Those who could get their battledress from the echelon put it on, as the nights were now bitterly cold and the dew was very heavy. Orders were given out. Troop Leaders were called to receive information from the Intelligence Officer, Second-Lieutenant Muir. He told of our forces, of how and where they would attack, and what they would achieve. He gave us the composition of 30th Corps. "Information about the enemy," he said, "is contained in Appendix 'A.' Unhappily, my dear chap, Appendix 'A' has still to reach us, so you must take my word for it." Devices to enable those captured to escape were handed to certain officers, and consisted of maps on handkerchiefs and tiny compasses concealed in buttons and pipes; maps as far as Tripoli, one thousand miles away, were issued and stowing them properly folded and in the right order in a crowded tank was not easy; nor did the problem of destroying them if one was captured appear simple. But at least it showed an optimistic High Command. The echelon was working frantically to catch up with its supply problem. Lieutenant Jerden, the Quartermaster, managed to get one day's rations and some water. Second-Lieutenant Cowan, in the dark, succeeded in getting some ammunition. The spare officers and crews who were to be left out of battle set off for the L.O.B.[1] Camp, but came back, as there was no transport to take them there. The Padre went round squadrons and celebrated Holy Communion—our first Service with no one between ourselves and the enemy, and, indeed, the last before we met him face to face. H.Q. Squadron Leader, Major Sinnott, and Captain Lloyd spent an anxious and sleepless night in their Staff car pondering on the fate of the Regiment going into its first battle without proper supplies. And the Prime Minister was to say later in the House of Commons, "everything was ready on the night of the 17th."

Early on the evening of the 17th, the 2nd in command, Major Mylne, and officers and N.C.O.'s from all regiments in the Brigade set out through the wire to make a petrol dump for the first re-fill next morning, so as not to take petrol from the Echelon. At 5 o'clock the Regiment close leaguered, and final orders were given out. The next few hours were spent by Troop Leaders, shut down in their tanks to conceal the light, struggling to sort out their maps and the mass of paper that it was considered necessary they should have. All the maps were never got out to Tank Commanders, but it did not matter, as it turned out, since only one was required till we were re-equipped. That night great flashes were seen to the north of us over SALUM and were thought at first to be the preliminary bombardment, but were finally, and correctly, assumed to be an electric storm.

The encirclement and destruction of the enemy armour and subsequently the rest of his forces, for such was General Cunningham's plan, was based principally on the speed and fire power of the British tanks. The 7th Armoured Division, consisting of three Armoured Brigades, the 22nd, 7th, and 4th, in that order from the left, was stationed at

[1] Left out of battle.

ADVANCE INTO ENEMY TERRITORY

the southern end of the line. Each Brigade was to advance north-west in a semicircle towards TOBRUCH; that heroic and weary garrison was to break out and join up; SIDI REZEGH aerodrome was to be captured, and the German and Italian armour forced to fight back for it with their supply line cut. The remainder of the British line was to attack and squeeze the enemy forces between themselves and 7th Armoured Division. The 22nd Armoured Brigade had the 4th County of London Yeomanry on the left, 2 R.G.H. in the centre, and 3rd County of London Yeomanry on the right, and when the advance commenced 2 R.G.H. led, with the 11th Hussars patrolling up to twenty miles in front. The Brigade was intended to take up a battle position at BIR DUEDAR, some eighty miles to the north-west.

* * *

At 6 a.m., on the morning of November 18th, the advance into enemy territory began. The Regiment moved off with H Squadron leading, F Squadron on the right, and G Squadron on the left. G Squadron were lucky to move at all as they had been given paraffin for their last re-fill; the R.A.S.C., however, sent their regrets. We might have been going on an exercise; there was no artillery barrage, no circling aeroplanes, none of the things associated with the opening of an offensive; and there was no enemy. Two hours brought us to the wire just south of Fort Maddalena. The gaps already made were quickly found and we streamed through into Libya. The Regimental Navigator, Lieutenant Snell, brought us straight to the petrol dumps, and above us now appeared a number of our fighters to prevent enemy interference while we filled up. By 10 a.m. we were under way again, with nothing in view but open, rolling desert, and the burnt-out framework of a crashed aeroplane standing on its nose. As we progressed the camouflage hoods began falling off and one by one were left in the sand, no doubt often helped by crews, till in the afternoon we looked almost like a Regiment of tanks again. Various unexplained delays occurred on the march, and during one of them we "brewed up," and by late afternoon were nearing our destination. Here Major Smail,[1] of the 11th Hussars, met us and told us of ten Italian M. 13 tanks five miles in front. F Squadron were sent forward to see if they could engage them quickly, and guns were loaded with the intention of killing somebody, if they were let off, for the first time. But they had vanished, and the Regiment close leaguered near BU SCIHAN, seventy-five miles from its starting point, without having seen any sign of the enemy we were supposed to be fighting. Several tanks had fallen out on the way, but some joined up early next morning.

It was known that there was an enemy strong point at BIR EL GUBI a few miles to the north-west, and that the Italian Ariete Division was close by, so, maintenance completed and tanks filled up, the Regiment went to sleep knowing that the morning would see its first battle. Everybody was in the best of spirits and perfectly confident of being able to deal with whatever force they were asked to take on. It has since been supposed, and indeed countenanced by the Home Government, that morale and Montgomery were God's gifts to the Eighth Army. The 8 on the Africa Star was awarded only to those who were in it at, and after, the last battle of El Alamein. The Eighth Army was formed in the summer of 1941, and was composed of British and Dominion Regular and Territorial troops, whose job it was to hold on while the rest got ready. They had their reverses, but also their victories. The spirit was there, but the guns were not. When the weapons came they did not stop till the Brenner and Luneberg Heath. The British, with their Australian, Indian, New Zealand, and South African comrades, can be excused for saying that without Wavell, without TOBRUCH, SIDI REZEGH, and KNIGHTSBRIDGE, and without the first battles of EL ALAMEIN,

[1] Major Smail had been Adjutant and had commanded A Squadron 1 R.G.H.

FIRST SHELLS BURST AMONGST US

"there wouldn't have been no last battle of Alamein nor no Africa Star." The Brigade Intelligence Officer had previously given us a talk on German and Italian tanks, and had said that the only tank that might bother us was the German Mk. IV, and that there were only twenty of them in North Africa. The German Mk. II and III and the Italian M. 13 would, he assured us, present no difficulties. We felt almost sorry for the enemy. That information, the fact that we felt well trained and had taken so long over it, and the inherent feeling in the British soldier that he can beat anybody, allowed us a night with fewer qualms than if we had known what we were to face next day.

At seven in the morning the advance was continued in the same order as on the previous day. A short halt was made at BIR DUEDAR and we continued towards BIR EL GUBI. There was no sign of the 3rd and 4th County of London Yeomanry or of Brigade H.Q., but they seemed satisfied with our position, though it appeared to us that we were alone in the desert. At 9.30 the Regiment had reached Point 181, where the Italians had planted a large red flag, and here an 11th Hussar armoured car met us and reported four Italian M. 13's to the north-west. Colonel Birley went over to their H.Q. nearby to discuss the situation. He dismounted and ran over to the Commanding Officer's car, his pipe and his chin sticking out—the warhorse scenting powder. Colonel Leatham greeted him with, "Now, Charles, don't you start a battle before these fellows have found my cigarette holder." Returning, he ordered H Squadron to attack. At this moment, shells began bursting amongst us, quite surprising us, and we realised we were not on an exercise this time. Those who had got out quickly jumped back into their tanks. Eighteen enemy tanks with artillery were reported to the north, and G Squadron was told to advance to assist H Squadron. However, as the 4th County of London Yeomanry who had suddenly appeared on our left, seemed to be attacking these same tanks, G Squadron waited, and Major Reinhold, H Squadron leader, reported at the red flag to say that he had knocked out six Italian tanks, but was not sure of his own casualties, though Second-Lieutenant Crossman had been heard on the air saying that his tank had been knocked out and his driver, Corporal South, killed. Major Reinhold later reported that Second-Lieutenant Honeysett and his complete crew had been killed as well as others; Lieutenant Elder Jones had lost an arm and a few others also had been wounded.

We were now told by Brigade to continue, so, as H Squadron could not be properly rallied, G Squadron took the lead, and Lieutenant Harper, looking out of his tank to get a sight of the general situation, was shot through the head from the ground and killed instantly. H Squadron were to come in on the left, and F Squadron remained on the right. After passing through considerable shell-fire we came upon numerous slit trenches, some with small anti-tank guns, filled with Italians all holding up white handkerchiefs and doing their best to surrender. We were unable to deal with them, however, and pressed on, leaving them behind huddled in groups. Here we encountered some Italian lorries, which we shot up with our Besas, setting them on fire and causing two containing ammunition to explode. There now appeared to be no enemy in front of us, and we stopped for a breather and to collect ourselves. H Squadron had had a more difficult time, as the Italians opposite them had stuck to their guns, and they had lost some more tanks. They were told to collect and follow in our wake, but they did not in fact appear till later in the afternoon.

While waiting to go on, Corporal Harmer, G Squadron, came up and displayed four holes in his tank. This distressed us as we had not realised that our beautiful tanks could be penetrated so easily. Captain Paterson, G Squadron, wirelessed to say he was still in the infantry position

GERMAN 88 MM GUN
BIR EL GUBI

PICKING UP R.G.H. CASUALTIES
AT BIR EL GUBI

ADVANCE TO ENGAGE ENEMY TANKS

through which we had just passed, with a broken axle arm and surrounded by Italians. No help, however, could be sent. He remained there all day, his tank being repeatedly hit and finally catching fire. When, eventually, he and his crew, Lance-Corporal Oliver, Trooper Beard, and Trooper Morgan, baled out and tried to run for it they were surrounded and captured by Italians. During this part of the engagement, 2nd Lieutenant Gordon-Creed's tank had a track shot off. He continued, however, to circle on the other track and knocked out two Italian tanks at point blank range. His own tank was then hit again through the turret, and his gunner and wireless operator were wounded. When the action died down he and his driver, Trooper Parker, got out the injured men and dressed their wounds, staying with them until the Medical Officer picked them up. Then they returned to the tank and began repairing it under heavy fire. By working all through the night, in close proximity to the enemy, and with every chance of being captured, they were ready by dawn and brought the tank back to the Regiment; 2nd Lieutenant Gordon-Creed was awarded the M.C.

While we were still halted, seven misguided Italian M.13 tanks came toward us, making no attempt to engage. F Squadron and G Squadron, and R.H.Q. quickly turned their guns on them and put them out of action before they could return a shot. By now the wireless was giving trouble. H Squadron could not be heard, and Major Saleby, F Squadron, had to change tanks twice before he could come up on "send."

At about 1 p.m. a large force of enemy tanks was seen forming up to our north, and the Regiment, less H Squadron, advanced to engage them. As we drew nearer we could see that they were Italian M. 13's interspersed with German Mk. IV's, and numbered about one hundred and sixty. There was also an enormous gun in the background, which turned out to be an 88-mm., our first experience of that formidable weapon, which proved the most successful and troublesome gun of the war. We had the satisfaction of passing it derelict some weeks later. G Squadron was still leading, with F Squadron as protection right, and the enemy force split in two, one part remaining to take on G Squadron and the other moving round to tackle F. The 3rd County of London Yeomanry had been ordered to come up on our right and execute a flank attack, but were unable to do so, and we were left to deal with odds of five or six to one. The enemy now closed into a tight box formation and came slowly at us, halting at about three thousand yards. This was the signal for his gunners to put down a concentrated barrage, and it continued from then on. His tanks came on again, and at about two thousand yards engaged with armour-piercing shot. Shells banged and smacked against our tanks, and sand, dust, and smoke caused by high explosive made it impossible to follow clearly what was happening. But what was clear was the fact that the enemy could penetrate our tanks at fifteen hundred yards, whilst our shells were bouncing off his and continued to do so down to eight hundred yards. And this inequality of fire-power was to hamper us through the rest of the campaign. While trying to follow the trend of the battle, and keep one's gunner on a target, one caught glimpses of tanks smoking and on fire, of men jumping out of them, and running wildly to the cover of stationary vehicles through the dust and smoke and hail of high explosive shells. Other tanks, damaged, reversed away and, picking up the crews on the ground, crawled off towards the red flag from which they had started.

It was now obvious that those tanks that were left in action were heavily outnumbered and out-gunned, and the order to withdraw was given. It came through very faintly on the air, "'Next' will withdraw," and in a voice that did not sound authentic. Some thought it was a German station, but R.H.Q. was moving back, so those that could

LT-COL. BIRLEY WOUNDED

followed, slowly and in good order, firing over their tails. More crews were picked up on the way, and a halt was made to face the enemy again in the first infantry position. But our "prisoners" of the morning turned their guns on us, so we moved on quickly. Trooper Davies and Trooper Reynolds were killed on the outside of a tank, and Trooper Winstone wounded, but Sergeant Jeffes arrived in time to see the gun fire and, driving his tank straight at it, crushed both the gun and its crew.

The remnants of the Regiment collected at the red flag, and late that evening close leaguered and began to count what the day had cost.

Lieutenant-Colonel Birley's tank during the afternoon had run into another and broken a track. The Colonel climbed on to the outside of his rear link's tank (Second-Lieutenant Muir) and was wounded in the process. Though suffering from a broken arm and in great pain, he sat during the rest of the battle fully exposed and under intense fire, directing the Regiment. He refused to be evacuated till he had seen the Regiment withdraw and go into close leaguer, and had handed over to Major Mylne. Then he permitted himself to be taken to Brigade H.Q., where he slept the night in the back of the Padre's car. The following morning he was so insistent that he should return to the Regiment that the Padre was forced to get the Brigadier to order him to go back to hospital. He was awarded the D.S.O.

Trooper Furnivall and Trooper Vowden, driver operator and gunner respectively, were in the same tank when it was knocked out by an anti-tank gun and the driver killed. Every effort to remove the dead man failed, and the crew baled out and took cover on the ground. Trooper Furnivall refused offers by other tanks to take him to safety and remained by his tank under heavy fire. Later, still under heavy fire and assisted by Trooper Vowden, he returned to his vehicle, and, squeezing into the seat on top of the

2ND ROYAL GLOUCESTERSHIRE HUSSARS

dead driver, brought the tank to safety. For this he received the M.M.

Sergeant Carsley, F Squadron, when forced to bale out, hid with others in the scrub, and was lucky enough not to be spotted when the enemy over-ran the position. He walked all that night in an easterly direction, feeling it best to go toward our troops advancing from the wire. After lying up by day and walking by night through the enemy positions, picking up food and water from derelict vehicles, he eventually ran into British hands, tired and in an exhausted condition, and rejoined us later.

In all, thirty tanks had been lost, though ten damaged ones were got away under Lieutenants Pitman and Bourne and reached Brigade H.Q. next morning; two officers (Second-Lieutenant Honeysett and Lieutenant Harper) and eight other ranks were killed (Corporal South, Troopers Astbury, Cook, Davies D., Humphries, Hellings, McRae, and Reynolds). Sergeant Woodger died of wounds late in the day, and three officers (Lieutenant-Colonel Birley, Captain White and Lieutenant Elder Jones) and twelve men were wounded (Troopers Lee W., Morgan W., Winstone, Wilson, Wiggall, Armstrong, Chiswell, Mallow, Murrow, Smith K., White J. W.).

Of some of the twenty-five captured more can be told. Major Saleby, after the Italian Armistice, spent six months at liberty and made numerous attempts to get through to the Eighth Army lines, but was recaptured and sent to Germany. Lieutenant Clay, whose tank had broken down at the red flag early in the morning, was asked that evening by the Brigadier to go and find the Commanding Officer. Taking Lieutenant Bourne's tank and crew he proceeded in the direction of the battle in the failing light, and ran into an anti-tank position and was knocked out and captured. He mystified the Italians for a while as he was dressed entirely in civilian clothes. His driver, Trooper Parry, was wounded in the leg and sent to hospital in Bengasi, from

EXPERIENCES OF THOSE CAPTURED

where he was later liberated. Trooper Lapworth was also freed from hospital in Bengasi. Corporal Bates, with Trooper George, who had had his eye shot out, while trying to run back to safety, saw an abandoned Italian lorry. In this they drove to our tanks, but, finding the fire too hot for a soft vehicle, set off to try and find a first-aid post, and missing their direction they ran into an Italian machine-gun post and were captured. Trooper Wakefield was amongst those who, towards the end of the war, was put to work in the Polish mines and, on the approach of the Russians, took part in the three months' march across Germany in the depth of winter till freed by the Americans a few days before the end of the War. Trooper Waddell, who was also in this march, died during the course of it.

Captain Playne, with a Commando officer, made a successful but short-lived escape from a camp near Bari in Italy. The following day General Bellomo came to hold an inquiry, and took the two officers to the scene of their escape. There, in a fit of excited anger, he ordered the guards to fire on them. Captain Playne was killed instantly and the Commando officer wounded. He, however, recovered, and on returning to England reported the matter. General Bellomo was subsequently tried and shot for murder.

The others captured were Captain Paterson, Sergeant Clarke, Sergeant Havins, Corporal Craddock, Lance-Corporal Oliver, Troopers Beard, Carter, Morgan L., Parsons, Payne, Sims, Stagg, Johnson E., Staite, Wadley, and Webber.

But, to our credit, the enemy were reported to have lost seventy tanks, and though this was never confirmed, the Ariete Division did not again appear as a fighting force.

Lieutenant Elder Jones's account of the first part of this action is as follows:—

When the dust appeared I ran back to my tank. The Colonel made for his. Presently the frying-egg sound in the headphones ceased and the Commanding Officer's voice broke the long wireless silence. With the slight pauses between word-groups, which always indicated his excitement, he said, in a mixture of code and clear: "Orders. Seventeen M-Thirteens about to attack G frontally (pause) H Squadron will go round right flank and contain them (pause) Move now. Pipi over."

Like a flash Major Reinhold's voice came up: "Fide O.K. off. Fide Flick." The operator's hand shot out to the knob and changed the frequency. The voice came back: "Fide calling. Two up, Four left, Two right, One left, Three right, Conform to me. Off."

Douglas swung to his right and was away. The two rear troops now taking the lead rushed up and formed level with him, then the other two moved after them, about 800 yards behind. Douglas held his rightward course for some minutes behind the rise, then turned a right angle left. We ate up about a mile of the flat in this direction, going all out. We then turned another right angle to the left for the run in. It was exactly like the start of a point-to-point. From the moment when Charles's voice came up there was a slight turn in the pit of my stomach and a tendency to hold breath. When the flag went down, and we ran, the nervousness seemed to go and only an excitement, rather pleasant, remained.

On this last lap it warmed up, even for the rear troops. Shells were bursting about the place and bits of metal clonked against the tank. Then we saw them in front of us. No possible mistake. They must have turned off from G towards the County of London Yeomanry, and were now coming back and turning at us. No chance of counting them, too much dust. I thought they were brave coming at us. They must have known what their own tanks were worth and H mustered fifteen.

My troop had to go very slowly as the front line sat still shooting at them, and did not seem to come out quick

ACCOUNT OF ACTION

enough. Eventually I halted. It was unhealthy, for while we were out of our range, their guns were ranging on us, and there was a clatter of machine gun bullets on our starboard side. I could not account for this last fire, but, of course, it was the entrenched positions on our right.

There were German infantry there; I thought I saw a Jerry helmet on a man at one point, and Trooper J. Lee, who was out on the right, told me later he saw and had a shot at some Germans who were clearing out in troop carriers.

A sizeable shell burst right up to our tank. I got on the 'phone to Douglas and asked him if I could come up, as the front troops were still there. There was no reply, my aerial had been carried away. So I went up. The din was terrific, and the dust. It cleared a second and there was an M.13 400 yards off us. McRae fired twice and the M.13 was alight. Through the same clearing a long way back I saw some Jerries (by their hats) pushing an anti-tank gun around, but the murk closed up again. My driver kept moving. He did one circle and then something hit us. The 2-pounder went off twice at a distant M.13, which I don't think we hit. Corporal Enoch, the operator, relaying it from the driver, yelled:

"Track off, Sir."

"Driver, reverse off your track and go in circles," I replied down the inter-communication 'phone. There was another crash and the inter-communication was U.S.[1]

"Can't move, Sir. Track is jammed," Corporal Perry's voice came to me.

"All right. Keep your engine revving. Enoch, fire some smoke."

I popped my head out to see what could be seen; there was one of our tanks, a faint shape, moving back on the right of us. My head was in quickly, as the bullets were coming over like rain. A shell burst right under our front and the concussion knocked Corporal Perry pretty silly,

[1] Unserviceable.

as he must have been about two feet from it on the other side of the plate. I kept swinging the periscope. Suddenly a patch cleared and there was an M. 13 about forty yards off. My fire-order drill went to hell in a scream, "Gunner, traverse right, Wop, fifty yards." McRae swung round. Before he had completed the traverse there were two klonks to port, and the engine died out. Those two shells must have gone through the petrol tanks to get there, but the fuel did not light. McRae turned to the hand traverse. Enoch popped his head out to see the fun. The 2-pounder banged and a hole appeared in the Wop's side like a dinner plate. Enoch shouted, "We got him, Sir, by God we got him. That's two."

"Why, in hell, haven't you fired that smoke? Fire it."

Enoch told me afterwards that he could not because something had come through the front and wrapped the smoke mortar round the Besa breech, had gone over his head, through the box of hand grenades (at any rate they were fallen on the floor), through the wireless, and out through the back. It may be so. I never noticed it, although later I observed a big hole just under the mouth of the smoke mortar. It was imperative to get smoke down because, when the dust cleared, every anti-tank gun in Libya would be on us.

The fixed machine-gun fire was still coming at us; our gun was still traversed full right after the last shot. I had a moment to wave the "I am out of action" flag. It was knocked out of my hand. It would have been sense to abandon tank then, but unsafe because of the machine-gun fire, nor was I sure if the enemy were still about. There seemed to be some, as we were being hit constantly on the left by what sounded like anti-tank shells. This was partly so. What was hitting us was the overthrow fire of the 4th County of London Yeomanry, who were still blazing at the only enemy tank left from long range. Their shells stopped my engine. Suddenly the machine-gun fire ceased. Perry said: "If you are

ACCOUNT OF ACTION

abandoning, traverse so that I can raise my flap." Enoch said, because he knew about the smoke: "We are in a nasty spot, Sir." I distinctly remember saying with detached pomposity: "An extremely unpleasant situation," because I was listening to an engine running not far away.

"Gunner, traverse left."

"Target, Sir," requested McRae, who was a very precise gunner.

"I can't see yet, only hear him."

The hand traverse is slow. It had got nearly to 12 o'clock when it came to us, crash. The anti-tank shell hit the junction of the front and left side turret plates and penetrated. Poor McRae was killed instantly. My right arm, which was up to the periscope, fell to my side, and Enoch reported, "I'm hit, Sir."

"So am I. Abandon tank."

Another shell whizzed over my head as I got out, and for the last time nearly hanged myself by jumping down without first removing the earphones from my head.

I have always assumed it was that anti-tank gun I had seen which got me, but I don't know. The hole was a bit bigger than the Italian shell or our own. It came from that direction, and the hole looked like a 50-mm. There were three of our tanks which were casualties besides mine. They were a long way away. One had no turret on it.

The three other tanks referred to were those of Second-Lieutenant Honeysett and Sergeant Woodger, both of whom were killed, and Second-Lieutenant Gordon-Creed. Lieutenant Gordon-Creed lost a track early on. It was clean broke by a shell, and in his own words: "We roared round in a circle with two Wops chasing us. It was frightful, because my turret was traversing so fast I did not know which way I was facing, and every one was shooting at me, too damn close to hit each other." However, Second-Lieutenant Gordon-Creed cannot have been so confused as he makes out. Both the enemy tanks perished with all their crews before he stopped his gyrations. His driver was wounded and had his leg shattered. Trooper Lee was hit in the head by a machine-gun bullet when getting out. Second-Lieutenant Gordon-Creed dealt with the leg himself and did it so effectively that the medical men complimented his skill.

Corporals Perry and Enoch owed something to Trooper Lee, who, in spite of his shot head, took the anti-aircraft Bren off his tank and lay down on guard with it. ("I was pretty soft, but not much more than usual.")

The tank that I had heard came up to us. It spluttered and the engine stopped. Evidently it had been winged. I was lying on the ground with my elbow shattered, with Corporal Perry near me in a dazed condition. The Italians threw a grenade at us. Corporal Enoch, who was wounded and could not use his right arm, was some distance away. The Italians, two of them, came forward brandishing pistols and shouting. I was trying to put a tourniquet on my arm, but the wind had blown the silk handkerchief I would use out of reach. They were greasy, unkempt devils. I shouted, "Si parla Ingleese?" at one—all the Italian I knew—but he said he didn't. So I shouted more loudly, and in English, "Help me to put this bloody thing on," I pointed to the handkerchief. He picked up the handkerchief and gave it to me, but he turned green and trotted off to Enoch without doing more. They collected Enoch and Perry and pointed to me, and then to their tanks, and marched off. The idea was to look for any wounded.

Corporal Perry said it made him sick to look inside the M. 13's. None of the seventeen got home as far as he could count, and these were the only two men alive. During this performance, Trooper Lee took a shot at the two Italians and got them, so Perry and Enoch returned to me, who had meantime been picked up by the 11th Hussars, who, fortunately, had a doctor with them.

* * *

A BREW-UP

PRISONERS OF WAR—SIDI REZEGH

SIDI REZEGH

The following morning Major Mylne took command, and the nineteen tanks that were left were formed into one Squadron under Major Trevor. Contact was made with the Echelon that had come up to BIR BERRANEB. It had been bombed by Stukas and Trooper Doyle killed and was still having trouble with supplies, but it was keeping the tanks going in spite of difficulties.

At about noon the Brigade was ordered to go to the assistance of the 4th and 7th Armoured Brigades, who had been, and still were, having tremendous battles with the German armour near GABR SALEH. The rest of the day was spent trying to find them, and we did not reach them till late in the evening. Though tracer shells in the distance showed the battle was still raging, we did not become involved and went into leaguer.

The next day the Regiment was nearly in action at first light, but the enemy withdrew, and we were told to move towards BIR ER REGHEM. The advance was slow as we went through a stationary South African Brigade. This Brigade we were to meet two days later in less peaceful circumstances. At about 3 p.m. two or three tanks caught up having had repairs done at field workshops, and 22nd Armoured Brigade started a wide movement so as to come in on the flank of the battle that could be seen some miles away. During the march, black clouds filled the sky and a torrential downpour burst upon us, and as we neared the battle in the failing light tracer shells and gun flashes lit up the leaden sky and a dozen tanks were burning furiously between the opposing forces. We arrived too late to do anything but fire a few rounds into the murk and withdraw into leaguer, bedding down in soaking blankets in the eerie light cast by the flames from the burning tanks, which were found to be British Mk. IV's.

The following morning the Brigade concentrated in a battle position near SIDI REZEGH aerodrome, and we were replenished by A.1 Echelon. The situation was far from clear and did not look too hopeful, as 4th Armoured Brigade and 7th Armoured Brigade had been reduced to almost nothing the day before. There was a large number of German tanks about, and some gunners who were just in front of us said that they had already fired their guns to the north, west, and east that morning, and fully expected to be engaged from the south before long. While we were waiting occasional shells fell amongst us, and at one o'clock seventy German tanks appeared on the other side of the aerodrome. The Brigade was told to move forward on to a ridge and to prevent the enemy, who were on a ridge opposite, from getting on to it. They were about two thousand yards away and out of range of our guns, and we were subjected to heavy shelling, both high explosive and armour piercing, while on the aerodrome on our right derelict planes were bursting into flames and their ammunition exploding. We were now asked to move round between the two ridges and to attempt to outflank the enemy, but no sooner were we half-way than hidden machine and anti-tank guns opened a furious fire and forced us back. Major Trevor's tank was knocked out, but he and his crew were rescued by Captain Ling under cover of smoke. Captain Ling returned to the battle and, his internal communication breaking down, was unable to stop his driver, who drove full speed right over the anti-tank position and back again without being put out of action, though his tank was hit several times. Visibility became very bad and the action was broken off, the Regiment going into leaguer, only to be moved, just as tea was nearly ready, to protect the flank of the same South Africans we had met two days before. A bitter cold night was spent sitting up in our tanks with two members of every tank crew on the alert. The expected attack, however, did not materialise, and at dawn we were able to get our first meal since breakfast on the previous day.

We had scarcely finished when an armoured car from the 11th Hussars reported German tanks forming up

FACING 100 GERMAN TANKS

behind us, so we turned round to face south and we remained all the morning watching over a hundred German tanks some three miles away with a screen of anti-tank guns in front of them. No attempt was made either by guns or aircraft to molest them and only one of our planes was seen. On our left was the South African leaguer, which we had protected during the night, with infantry, 25-pounders, 2-pounders, and its complete Brigade Echelon of some one thousand vehicles. On our right it was supposed were 4th and 7th Armoured Brigades, and it was not known at the time that both of them had virtually ceased to exist. Not only had they had very heavy casualties in their great battles, but 4th Armoured Brigade had been attacked in leaguer the night before, and had evidently received the attack which we had expected on the South African leaguer. In fact only a few Mk. IV Cruiser tanks of 2nd Royal Tank Regiment were left, and had we realised that we were practically the only armour left to deal with this mass of German tanks in front of us our spirits would have been lower than they were. For our spirits were low. We knew now that the German tanks outnumbered and outgunned us and had thicker armour; that they were fighting the battle the way they wanted it fought and had caused our plans to go badly astray. We had been fighting them for nearly a week, had suffered heavy casualties, and had been forced to withdraw every time we had met them. And now there were a hundred of them quietly refuelling three miles away.

During the morning, as the Germans did not seem to be coming on, the Brigade was reformed into three Squadrons, 2 R.G.H. Squadron being commanded by Major Trevor. As there were thirteen officers in seventeen tanks, some of them were ordered to return to the Echelon, and about lunch-time Major Mylne, Major Reinhold, and Lieutenants Adlard, Snell, and Pitman, with two broken-down tanks and a scout car, set off. On reaching the South African leaguer they found H Squadron fitters and set about trying to get the tanks repaired. This, however, was interrupted by intense and accurate shell fire on the leaguer, and they remained pinned down in the open till escape was essential to avoid capture by German infantry who were forming up to overrun the position. Major Mylne and Major Reinhold got away in the scout car and Lieutenant Pitman, H Squadron fitters, and anybody who could crowd into it escaped in H Squadron fitters' 15-cwt., the dummy aerial of which was shot off one foot above the cab by a passing German shell to the consternation of those in the back. Lieutenant Snell and two members of one of the tanks were captured, while Lieutenant Adlard went back towards the Regiment in the other.

Meanwhile, the German tanks had disappeared for the purpose of splitting up out of sight, which enabled them to attack the South African leaguer from the south-east and east as well as the south-west. Shelling increased and vehicles in the leaguer were burning fiercely. The air was full of smoke and dust and the smell of cordite. A large gun opened fire from behind, and though two tanks from 2nd Royal Tank Regiment went to silence it they were never seen again. German tanks were coming into the leaguer from the south-west, but in no apparent hurry, and the Regiment spent the next hour advancing on them in short rushes, firing and coming out again. By now Brigade H.Q. and the rest of the Brigade had vanished, wireless contact had been lost, and lack of information and orders made it impossible to know what to do. The German armour was coming in from the south and south-west, German infantry from the north and north-east, and fire of every sort was pouring in from every side. The leaguer was a shambles. Hundreds of vehicles were burning, and those that could still move were trying to get out as best they could. The South African gunners, those that were left, were firing at point-blank range at German tanks till they were overrun and killed and could fire no

GERMAN MARK IV
KNOCKED OUT AT SIDI REZEGH

CRUSADER
KNOCKED OUT AT SIDI REZEGH

ESCAPE FROM SOUTH AFRICAN LEAGUER

more. The Regiment tried to rally at the north-west corner, but only about six tanks arrived. A move was made to the north-east side to try and deal with the infantry attack, but it was supported by guns and tanks. Lieutenant Bourne's tank was knocked out, and Lieutenant King had his 2-pounder barrel shot off. Lieutenant Cookson rescued the Colonel and 2nd in command of 4th County of London Yeomanry, and his tank, though penetrated in the radiator, managed to get them to safety.

Light had now failed, and the blackness was lit up by tracer bullets, shell-fire, and burning and exploding trucks. The two H.Q. Troop tanks linked up with Captain Ling and Captain Hart, and Lieutenant King with his crew and Lieutenant Bourne arrived on foot. Lieutenant Adlard appeared with a 15-cwt. truck towing a 25-pounder which he had got from the South Africans, and the party set off through the burning vehicles trying to find a way out. But this proved impossible, and it was decided to wait till the moon went down, unless discovery by the Germans forced a move sooner. During the wait, Second-Lieutenant Muir's operator managed to get contact with Brigade H.Q., who gave their position, and Captain Ling worked out the bearing and distance. A German column passed within one hundred and fifty yards, but did not discover the tanks, and a South African armoured car joined the group. Then, as the moon went down about midnight, the sentries were called in, engines started, and the party moved off. Seldom have six vehicles moved faster, and there was no slackening till the Germans and the South African leaguer were left well behind. When a halt was called there was no sign of the armoured car or the 15-cwt. and 25-pounder. The move was then continued at a more normal pace with Captain Hart's tank on tow till Brigade H.Q. was reached.

Lieutenant Adlard, with his truck and 25-pounder, was taken prisoner, and was awarded the M.C. on the recommendation of the South Africans. Finding the

Regiment when he left the leaguer in the afternoon, but being disabled, he spent the rest of the battle with the South Africans, spotting enemy tanks for their gunners under intense shell-fire, ignoring great personal danger and the opportunity to escape in trucks that were getting out.

Lieutenant King also won the M.C. for towing out tanks under heavy fire and for great courage and initiative in fighting his own tank. Lance-Sergeant Anderson received the M.M. for towing out a tank and its crew under heavy fire and at considerable personal risk.

In this battle, miraculously, only Trooper Young was killed, and only Trooper Pearce wounded. His tank had its sprocket shot off, and Trooper Pearce's feet were injured. He was got to a first-aid post by Lieutenants King and Bourne, and during the next day was captured and re-captured as one side or the other got possession of the dressing station. Finally, it was captured once again by his own side and he was rescued.

The prisoners lost were Lieutenant Adlard and Lieutenant Snell, Corporal Gardner D., Corporal Otterburn, Lance-Corporal Nunn, Troopers Bowers, Chalkley, Ellis O., Heggie, Porter, Smith, Tibbles, Mallon, and Sims. Second-Lieutenant Skinner was taken during the afternoon on coming up from the echelon to try to find a tank for himself. Sergeant Caudle was thought to be missing, but had been "captured" by the 5th Royal Tank Regiment when his tank was knocked out. In spite of his protests he was made to command a tank with them for two days. Having found out where the R.G.H. were, at a suitable moment, he handed over to the operator, raised his hat, and walked back to his Regiment. Of these prisoners, Corporal Gardner, Lance-Corporal Nunn, Troopers Sims, Ellis, Heggie, Bowers, and Chalkley, together with a few others, were marched for three and a half days without food or water, eventually reaching Bengasi. Here they were joined by Lance-Corporal Wright, and Trooper

"MOVE IN FIVE MINUTES"

Loveridge, who was captured a day later from the Echelon. With the addition of some captured at Bir el Gubi they sailed in an Italian ship for Italy battened down in the hold. When nearing Greece an R.A.F. plane spotted them and, not realising what the ship contained, reported its presence to a submarine, which torpedoed it. The Italian crew deserted the ship forthwith, and, though badly holed, it drifted ashore, and the R.G.H. prisoners were able to land safely, though some six hundred of the total complement were lost. The next few months were spent in Greece enduring terrible cold and privations till they were moved to Italy in March the following year.

On the next day, November 24th, Majors Mylne and Reinhold, Captain Hart, and Lieutenants King, Bourne, Cookson, and Pitman went back to B Echelon with surplus crews. Captain Brenchley (Technical Adjutant), Captain Waters (Medical Officer), and Second-Lieutenants Lawton and Crossman also joined the Echelon. They were given a good breakfast, razors, washing things, spare socks, and shirts, and anything else they wanted, and were treated more than generously, the Echelon crews going short themselves to provide for them. Just as they had settled down to a morning of relaxation the order came through "Move in five minutes." Captain Lloyd and Squadron Sergeant-major Summerell came round in a staff car to get everyone moving, and almost at the same moment German tanks appeared a thousand yards to the left and began shelling. Major Sinnott wheeled the Echelon to conform with Brigade Echelon, but some of F Squadron vehicles got caught and knocked out. There was some confusion at the suddenness of the German appearance, and owing to other echelons being forced amongst us and across our path. This caused vehicles to get split up into separate parties and, with a German column of unknown size containing tanks close upon us and shelling us, all speed was made in an easterly direction. Second-Lieutenant Ades, who had the wheel of his scout car off, replaced it in less time than he considered possible, and caught up one of the parties.

The rest of the day was spent travelling at a great pace towards the wire, with no orders and no information as to what was happening. Not even an armoured command vehicle, which was overhauled with difficulty, could explain. Frequent halts were made, but immediate shell-fire hustled us on. At nightfall the various parties except one, which, with the Padre and Lieutenant King, had managed to rejoin Brigade H.Q., crawled through the gaps in the wire that they had gone through so hopefully a week before in the other direction, and leaguered in Egypt, feeling that the Eighth Army had disintegrated and the war was lost. German tanks were heard leaguering just on the Libyan side of the wire only a short distance away.

The main party that had reached the LIBYAN SHEFERZEN gap earlier ran into a column of German motorized infantry on the same evening, which opened fire. The party immediately moved forward, but Major Sinnott's driver was wounded and he himself shot in the chest. As the operator was getting the injured driver out, a German jumped in and drove the truck away. The driver, Trooper Platt, died shortly after, and Lance-Corporal Jones, the operator, wounded in the arm, having buried him, was picked up by Indians, after hiding for twenty-four hours amongst the Germans. Major Sinnott died of his wounds in German hands, a great loss to the Regiment, in which he had been for seventeen years.

The same day at Sheferzen a number were captured, including Lieutenant (Quartermaster) Jerden, Squadron Sergeant-major Lee, Regimental Quartermaster Sergeant Barnes, Troopers Rudge and Phillips, and in a different party Captain Lloyd, Squadron Sergeant-major Summerell, Troopers Tuck, Petra, and Wood were taken while moving with Rear 30th Corps towards SIDI SULEIMAN by a German column that came out from HALFAYA.

PRISONERS ESCAPE FROM HALFAYA

The remainder of the Echelon proceeded on the morning of November 25th through main Eighth Army H.Q. to railhead, leaguering near it that night, and had the pleasure of seeing a train-load of German prisoners bombed by their own planes. Two days were spent at railhead collecting everybody who could be found, and then a move was made to the forward area again.

Meanwhile, Captain Lloyd, Lieutenant Jerden, Regimental Quartermaster Sergeant Barnes, Squadron Sergeant-major Summerell, and seventeen others who had been captured and had joined up with them, had been left under guard near Halfaya and had managed to persuade their two Austrian sentries to accompany them back to their own lines. With Squadron Sergeant-major Summerell navigating and carrying all the water they could, they walked twenty-four miles during the night and reached our troops next morning, and then came into railhead. But Squadron Sergeant-major Lee, Corporal Looker, Troopers Phillips, Cull, Woods, Merritt, Gledhill, and Gagg were not so lucky. They were taken to Halfaya, and confined there till it was captured by British troops. To keep out of our shell-fire, they made dug-outs in the side of a wadi; they were unable to wash for three weeks; they had no bedding or blankets and rations were bad and getting worse; they bartered for a cigarette, putting it in a pipe and passing it round. A shell landed amongst them and killed Trooper Gledhill, and a plan to escape was foiled by some Indians who got away first, causing the Germans to increase their precautions. Just before Christmas they were twice ordered to the beach to be taken off, but on the first night no boat arrived, and on the second it grounded in Salum Bay and was pounded to pieces by our artillery next morning; Squadron Sergeant-major Lee was slightly wounded by a splinter from one of our own bombs. The German Commander, when approached, allowed them to mark their position with water cans and gave them

2ND ROYAL GLOUCESTERSHIRE HUSSARS

a few blankets and overcoats from dead Germans. Nevertheless rations were getting still worse, and they were becoming very weak from lack of food and water, and realised that the end would come one way or the other soon. But their ordeal was closing. The Italian strong points began coming in and on January 17th, 1942, the garrison surrendered. The party rejoined the Regiment the following month.

While the Echelon was suffering its unpleasant experiences on November 24th, Lieutenant Bourne and Second-Lieutenant Wigley, finding some new tanks going up quite unaware that the Germans were loose in the desert, took over two of them and endeavoured to reach the Regiment. On their way they became protection to 7th Armoured Division H.Q., and then were told to convoy four hundred New Zealand lorries to their Division on the TRIGH CAPUZZO. Things did not go well and they spent most of their time repairing mechanical faults, till finally German tanks discovered them and they were captured. Lieutenant Bourne infuriated the monocled German officer by offering him sheets of toilet paper when asked for his "papers."

On November 24th, the tanks of the Brigade were formed into two weak Squadrons, Major Trevor commanding 2 R.G.H., and, accompanied by a battery of 25-pounders, they moved a few miles west to engage a column of enemy transport. It withdrew, however, and covered its withdrawal with an anti-tank gun which blew off Lieutenant Milvain's air cleaner. Two German Mk. II tanks assisted the anti-tank gun, and the column got away. That evening five Honey tanks, five Crusaders under Second-Lieutenant Gordon-Creed, and a Squadron of Mk. IV Cruisers from 2nd Royal Tank Regiment joined up.

The next two days were quiet, and a few tanks were salvaged from the battlefield and put in running order, but on the 27th a strong enemy column was reported moving along the Trigh Capuzzo towards Tobruch. The

SIDI REZEGH AGAIN

position there was still precarious, and to allow the link-up with our forces to be completed it was essential for this column to be delayed. When the enemy saw us he immediately sent out his tanks and anti-tank guns and began shelling. The Regiment worked round a flank, but ran into more anti-tank guns and had to withdraw, Lieutenant Milvain's track being shot off. He and his driver, Corporal Jones, managed to repair it under fire without being hit. Second-Lieutenants Gordon-Creed and Muir, on patrol, succeeded in getting round the enemy tanks and destroying some transport, but could not stay there long, and then the Germans came forward, giving our 2-pounders a chance. Second-Lieutenant Williams's tank was hit and burst into flames, but he and his crew escaped on foot. The attack was not pressed home, and the Regiment moved into leaguer.

The next morning a move was made to Bir er Reghem and an enemy force contacted. Captain Ling and his troop managed to patrol right up to them unseen and reported seventy tanks and a lot of guns. Later Captain Ling had his track knocked off by high explosive fire, but he and his crew were able to rejoin on foot. In the afternoon a junction was made with 4th Armoured Brigade, who had collected some more tanks, and a long range battle ensued, causing very little damage to either side. For the first time British air support was seen in operation, a dozen Blenheims bombing the enemy formation. This was the only occasion during the campaign that our planes gave the Brigade direct support. On the 29th we found ourselves at Sidi Rezegh again and saw what we had been hoping for so long, the invading British Army; there were troops and guns everywhere, coming up from the east. The following morning the Regiment was ordered south to join the Echelon and to refit.

Lance-Sergeant Jeffes received the M.M. for consistent initiative and courage under difficult circumstances during all this time. His tank was hit in several places at the battle of Bir el Gubi and from then on was virtually a crock. It was hit again in subsequent actions and suffered from smashed bogey wheels, leaking radiators, and other troubles. Nevertheless, Sergeant Jeffes and his crew kept it going for the best part of eleven days, often not being able to keep up and get into leaguer at night. But he turned up for every battle, and was always to the front in spite of the grave possibility of breaking down in the face of the enemy. Trooper Huxford was also awarded the M.M. for keeping his scout car close to the tanks at all times, frequently under heavy fire, carrying *liaison* officers, fitters, and others to all parts of the battlefield. Captain Ling, for his initiative and courage, whether as 2nd in command of a Squadron or Squadron Leader, for rescuing crews under heavy fire, for being invariably closer to the enemy than anyone else, and for fighting his tank on one track till that was shot off and his tank could not move, received the M.C. Major Trevor who had, with such ability, with such an offensive spirit, and with such cool and clear-headed calmness led the Regiment in whatever form it existed for most of this time, received the D.S.O. No matter how desperate the situation, without information or instructions, his personal courage and disregard for danger, his unerring judgment and clear orders made him the cornerstone upon which the Regiment built the reputation it earned during these battles.

* * *

On December 1st the whole Regiment had met at Point 172 some miles south-east of Bir el Gubi. They remained there for nine days, resting and reforming. Though water was scarce—only a quarter of a gallon a day per man, instead of half a gallon, ever arrived owing to leaking cans—general appearances changed quickly. Men were washed, shaved, in clean clothes, and well rested, and though rations were short it was something to have meals at regular intervals. On the 5th it was decided that the Regiment should have Honey tanks, and the job of sorting out and making up crews was begun. Casualties—

DE-SANDING

EL AMIRIYA—MERSA MATRUH EXPRESS

To face page 35

H.Q. NEAR KNIGHTSBRIDGE

sixteen officers and seventy other ranks—had to be made up, and the tanks were forced to have every available man from the Echelon while they made do as best they could. Two days later the tanks arrived. They had been 8th Hussar tanks and had fought many battles; they had all reached or passed their allotted mileage and had no tools, spares, or internal communication. Nevertheless, by the afternoon of the 9th, under the command of Major Trevor, Major Mylne[1] having been evacuated with concussion, the Regiment with fifty-two Honeys and a complete B Echelon, moved fifty-six miles north-west to 7th Armoured Division H.Q., passing through a large formation in open leaguer, which caused several tanks to get separated, and spend the night by themselves. The following day H Squadron were put on transporters and sent to join Lieutenant-Colonel Currie with a column of the Support Group.[2] In the afternoon two Messerschmitts attacked out of the sun at about fifty feet, setting on fire a petrol lorry and unfortunately killing Sergeant White. Then after leaguering the night, the Regiment, less H Squadron, moved on to join the Support Group H.Q.[3] near Knightsbridge, a scrub-covered, wind-swept piece of desert that became as well known as its London namesake some months later. A further move was made twelve miles west, where a G Squadron patrol reported twenty-four Italian tanks. Major Trevor and Second-Lieutenant Muir went to look at them, but were fired on and withdrew. There had been some shelling during the afternoon, but we leaguered at night without having been seriously molested.

[1] Major Mylne died in England as a result of blood poisoning which came to him from sores contracted in the desert.
[2] They were away two days trying to intercept the coast road near Gazala One enemy tank was knocked out. Unfortunately no records were kept.
[3] The Support Group at this time consisted of four columns of all arms operating separately. Their role was to harass enemy positions round GAZALA and TMIMI, while the New Zealand Division and 4th Indian Division came in from the east. Our own role was never clearly defined, but we were a force that Brigadier Campbell, V.C., the Support Group Commander, kept in reserve should any suitable target present itself.

35

2ND ROYAL GLOUCESTERSHIRE HUSSARS

Early on the morning of the 12th we again moved twelve miles west to a position known as "Double Blue." The enemy were in considerable strength in rocky, broken ground just to the west of us. Shortly after our arrival we received orders to do a demonstration in force along the southern edge of their position. Almost as soon as we had started we were subjected to intense, sustained, and accurate shell-fire, but though wireless aerials, blankets, and other kit were holed and in some cases blown off the tanks, none was hit, and after a run of twelve miles a halt was called. We then returned, making a somewhat wider sweep, but drew the same fire as on the way out. Corporal Poole inadvertently ran his tank into a swamp, but fortunately had enough way on to get through it without becoming bogged. H Squadron rejoined in leaguer the same evening.

On the 13th we were shelled just after breaking leaguer and Trooper Clark was wounded. The shell burst twelve yards from his tank on rocky ground, and the rest of the crew were lucky to escape unhurt. As a result of the information we had discovered the day before, that the enemy position was in some depth and was a strong point, we were told to do another similar demonstration in force, but this time to go right round the rear of the enemy. We were to fill up on the way. We set off about noon, and went much farther south to avoid the shell-fire, and after fifteen miles stopped in broken country to fill up. We had just started this operation when twelve Stukas appeared circling very low overhead, evidently forming up preparatory to going on a raid. That they saw us there can be no doubt, and it can but be assumed that they thought we were "Panzers," for they did not molest us, but a very uncomfortable quarter of an hour was spent fearing that they would drop their bombs. From this point we turned north to go behind the enemy, G Squadron left, F Squadron centre, and H Squadron right. We had not gone far when G Squadron ran into an anti-tank position in the escarpment

SHORT BUT HEAVY ENGAGEMENT

for which we were heading, and became heavily engaged. At the same moment, F and H Squadrons came upon a large amount of transport which they forced to move off in a disorderly hurry, setting several trucks on fire. More anti-tank guns were quickly unhitched from behind the lorries and came into action. They had the benefit of the rocky escarpment, while we were in the open, and as the American wireless sets were not working properly it was virtually impossible for Major Trevor to keep control. After thirty minutes furious shooting, under extremely heavy and accurate high explosive and armour piercing fire from the enemy, the Regiment withdrew at speed and rallied, being bombed by the same Stukas in the process. Casualties were heavy. Nine tanks were lost and left on the battlefield. Sergeant Constable, Sergeant Jeffes, Corporal Haines, and Troopers Collier and Harnden were killed. Troopers Chew, Hoskin, Rich, Wilkinson, Woods, Dimambro, and Townsley were wounded; and Corporal Harmer, Corporal Randall, and Troopers Booy and Pool, and a 3rd County of London Yeomanry crew that had been lent to us were captured. It was afterwards said that this action, small and brief though it was, materially assisted in persuading the enemy to withdraw from his strong position in that area.

During this battle, Trooper Rich and crew were forced to abandon their tank when it was hit and caught fire. As the flames appeared to abate Trooper Rich returned to it and tried to get it away, but was burnt in the face and had to give up. At that moment Major Reinhold drove up in his tank to rescue the crew, but had his own vehicle hit and his driver killed. The tank failed to stop and carried on with the dead driver in the seat. Trooper Rich sprang on to it, forced his way into the driving compartment, and drove the tank and both crews to safety. His quick action, though suffering considerable pain, in extremely unpleasant circumstances, saved the lives of his Troop Leader and crew and of Major Reinhold and his operator

2ND ROYAL GLOUCESTERSHIRE HUSSARS

and gunner. On his return to leaguer he was evacuated to hospital. He received the M.M.

Trooper Drake was also given the M.M. His tank was knocked out by an anti-tank gun, his commander killed, and the gunner very seriously wounded in the arm, which was later amputated. Trooper Drake immediately took command of the situation and directed the tank out of danger. At the same time he put a tourniquet on the gunner's arm and so certainly saved his life. He then went to the Regimental Navigator, Second-Lieutenant Boyd, and got directions from him to the starting point, where was the nearest medical aid. With no compass, but steering by the sun, he completed twenty miles on three separate legs. By determination and coolness in very trying circumstances he saved his crew and his tank, and got the gunner to a doctor in the shortest possible time.

Next morning H Squadron were again sent off, this time to the 22nd Guards Brigade, to carry out "an offensive sweep westwards," and they left on transporters just after dawn.[1] Later that morning the remainder of the Regiment moved eight miles north-east and joined 4th Armoured Brigade under Brigadier Gatehouse. There we learned that the plan to be put into operation was a vast out-flanking move which aimed at cutting off the entire enemy rearguard. 4th Armoured Brigade was to go twenty-one miles south, thirty miles west, and thirty miles north to BIR HALEGH EL ELEBA, and shortly after mid-day we set off with 3rd Royal Tank Regiment leading, 5th Royal Tank Regiment right, and 2 R.G.H. left, supported by 2nd Royal Horse Artillery and the Northumberland Hussars (Anti-tank Regiment). That night we leaguered at BIR ZEIDAM and filled up from the A.1 Echelon, which performed its nightly miracle of finding us in the dark.

[1] Again no records were kept. But the offensive sweep took place south of Bengasi to Antelat and beyond. Major Reinhold was killed on December 23rd, the only casualty sustained, and the Squadron, commanded by Second-Lieutenant Crossman, rejoined the Regiment on December 29th.

THE PADRE AND TECHNICAL ADJUTANT

Under Second-Lieutenant Lawton, the A.1 Echelon failed on no single occasion to come into the leaguer with supplies—petrol, ammunition, rations, water, the fitters, and, above all, the mail—unless the state of the battle was such that it was impossible to make the journey. The task of finding the tanks in leaguer, a target of less than a hundred square yards, in the pitch dark with no lights whatever, given only the bearing and distance and often having to cover many miles, was one of immense difficulty. It was quite possible to pass within fifty yards of the tanks and not see them, and equally possible to arrive at the wrong leaguer and fail to appear till next morning, when it was too late to refill. But this never occurred. The Padre, as there was no room for him in a tank, always came up with A.1 Echelon to see us. He used to chat to as many people as possible and bring us news and gossip. He always managed to seem to come from a different world and to take our minds off our unpleasant and uncomfortable duties, as though he had just come from Gloucestershire. "Doc" Waters and Captain Brenchley, the Technical Adjutant, also travelled officially in A.1 Echelon, though they used to plough across the desert as close to the tanks as they could, nor were they deterred by shot or shell. It was comforting to think that expert hands and the morphia needle were not far away, and tanks had their ailments diagnosed and their cure prescribed almost before their commanders had worked out their positions on the map.[1]

We pursued our advance next day and found the most atrocious going over the third leg, to the north. The tanks were reduced to walking pace, and the crews suffered badly from being thrown about inside their vehicles. We reached our objective without meeting any opposition, but that night in leaguer enemy Verey lights were going

[1] The Regimental Signals, who were Middlesex Yeomanry under Sergeant Byers, were also in A.1 Echelon and came up every night to deal with wireless troubles in leaguer. The L.A.D. (Light Aid Detachment) under Lieutenant Ibbott, worked in B Echelon, and tanks that the fitters could not repair went back for it to deal with.

up all round us. But they were not aware of intruders in their midst, and we were not discovered. The enemy, however, withdrew north of us during the night, making it impossible to cut them off, so we returned to the Echelons in the morning and then moved on to try and contact the enemy rearguards. During the march, while passing through a rocky defile, with the whole Brigade perfectly placed for enemy bombers, two Messerschmitts flew over and, evidently thinking we were their own side, came down to one hundred feet and circled over us, waving. Fortunately, nobody let his enthusiasm and excitement get the better of him, and no shot was fired till both planes were well placed, and then a positive hail of bullets was loosed upon them. For once the anti-aircraft Browning machine guns behaved quite well, and one was shot down crashing fifty yards from the Brigadier, while the other turned for home, tracer bullets tearing through its wings. Several derelict trucks were set on fire by Lieutenant King, and then the expected Stukas appeared, put on to us by the surviving Messerschmitt. We were heavily bombed, but luckily after we had emerged from the defile and were well spread out, and no damage was done. For the remainder of the afternoon the enemy shelled us from his positions amongst rocky wadis and 2nd Royal Horse Artillery replied, but no serious armoured engagements took place, though 3rd and 5th Royal Tank Regiments had a skirmish with enemy rearguards, the Regiment acting as protection left. Early on the 17th F Squadron, accompanied by a troop of anti-tank guns, was sent out alone towards TMIMI to see whether there was any sign of the enemy or of our own troops advancing along the coast. No enemy were seen, though several deserted trucks were set on fire. At about mid-day the leading troop sent back a worried message which inferred that both 15th and 21st Panzer Divisions were bearing down upon it. However, it turned out that it was 4th Indian Division, led by some Infantry tanks advancing through the dust and

CHRISTMAS DAY IN PEACE

mirage. The desert to the east was swarming with troops and equipment of every description, and there were more 4.5 guns than we thought existed. We had never, as spectators seen a Division on the move, and as it passed in front of us in open formation, each vehicle leaving a cloud of sand in its wake, creating a general haze that darkened the sky, we felt that we might get to Tripoli after all. And our optimism was not dimmed by capturing at that moment an Italian ration lorry. This contained, apart from five terrified Italians, tinned goods of various kinds, bags of sweets that assisted in warding off thirst, bottles of lemon juice, twenty gallons of brandy, and twenty-five gallons of pure water; and the thought of unlimited pure water for a day or two instead of the daily ration of a quarter of a gallon of warm salty water full of sand rejoiced our hearts. Rations at this time had dwindled to practically nothing, and were only coming up in a trickle, so the capture was doubly welcome. The truck also contained some hand grenades with a very uncertain safety device. After an understandably long halt, the Squadron set off back to the Regiment, but failed to find it that night, and after leaguering by itself, rejoined next morning. On the 18th orders were received to proceed to EL MECHILI to await the arrival of 22nd Armoured Brigade.

We were fortunate to pick on a leaguer area close to a lake with water fit for drinking, and so were able to fill up every available container as well as wash ourselves and our clothes. We maintained our tanks and turned over the tracks which were getting very worn, and on December 23rd moved off, leading the Brigade to SAUNNU, one hundred miles to the west, where we arrived on Christmas Eve. On Christmas Day we were left in peace and regaled ourselves with tea, bully beef and biscuits, and some of our Italian rations as a savoury. The news that Major Trevor had been awarded the D.S.O. gave him a well-merited Christmas present, and great pleasure to the Regiment, but a message that Major Reinhold had been killed two days before filled us with sadness. On Christmas Day the Padre gave a Service to the Echelon. The tanks, life being so uncertain, had had theirs on the Sunday before Christmas at El Mechili. We gathered round the Padre's sand-coated car with our tanks as a background, and, for a moment, forgot the difficulties and unpleasantness of life.

The plan was for 22nd Armoured Brigade, having received supplies, to cut the coast road as had been done the year before, and on the 26th we moved ninety-five miles south-west, passing to the east of AGEDABIA. In the evening, 3rd County of London Yeomanry engaged an enemy column, and F Squadron fired a few rounds into the dusk, and we leaguered ten miles short of our objective, CHOR ES SUFAN. On the 27th we moved two miles beyond Chor es Sufan to CHUER ESC SCIAH, where 3rd and 4th County of London Yeomanry were involved in a static and long-range battle with twenty-six enemy tanks; 2 R.G.H., watching the right flank, were not involved, but were intermittently shelled all day.

The following morning the Brigade took up the same position as on the previous day, and this was the first proper hull down position that we had had during the campaign. The enemy had six tanks on the ridge in front, and there was very considerable movement on the Agedabia track to our west, from first light. This increased as the morning wore on and more transport and guns could be seen. They started shelling us with some vigour and our own guns, for reasons best known to themselves, did not reply, although the enemy presented a magnificent target. Later in the day, when the situation was getting desperate, Lieutenant King was sent by Major Trevor to implore them to open fire, but without authority, they said, they could do nothing. So the enemy were permitted to shell us to their hearts' content all day and were never molested themselves. In the middle of the morning twenty-seven enemy tanks appeared to our front, and the shelling from

SUNDAY BEFORE CHRISTMAS DAY, 1941

COMMANDING OFFICER'S HONEY NEAR EL MECHILI

LONG AND TIRING NIGHT MARCH

the right increased in violence. By afternoon, the German tanks had increased in number and some fifty attacked, but at long last we had a good hull down position and their advantage in the range of their guns was largely offset, though their thicker armour still made it difficult to knock them out. But we were forced to withdraw to the ridge behind us, and for a time the enemy did not come on. We had by now lost touch with Brigade, and the enemy column to the west began to move round our right rear. Late in the afternoon the shelling increased still more and the German tanks advanced. With the assistance of the 3rd County of London Yeomanry they were held off, but the threat of encirclement was rapidly increasing, and finally we were all forced to withdraw in a hurry through the fast narrowing gap. The enemy guns lengthened their range and kept on shelling us with accurate violence for some time. The tanks were now very nearly out of petrol and in danger of coming to a standstill within easy reach of the enemy, so an urgent message was sent for a refill. This was picked up by the enemy and just as we halted to fill up from a passing petrol lorry, which, though nothing to do with us, was kind enough to supply us, we were heavily bombed by Stukas sent over for the express purpose of catching us in that vulnerable situation. No damage, however, was done, except that Sergeant Greaves was thrown with great violence to the bottom of his tank and suffered from blast. We withdrew then still farther and took up a position to protect the Echelon. But the enemy did not press home his attack, and we moved again by nightfall.

After a long and very tiring night march we leaguered and replenished. Casualties, though not as heavy as in some previous battles, were bad enough, and the loss of so many officers and men during the campaign and the physical and mental strain were beginning to tell. Second-Lieutenant Mitchell, Sergeant Rumsey, and Trooper How were killed; Trooper Patchett was missing and subsequently died as a prisoner. Troopers Brewster, Jones J., Marks, and Martin were made prisoners, and Second-Lieutenant Williams, Troopers Kemp, Leese, Rowarth, and Phillips wounded.

The next day we moved forward again, but had no contact with the enemy. H Squadron, commanded now by Second-Lieutenant Crossman, rejoined us and F Squadron helped to pull some County of London Yeomanry tanks out of a marsh. We leaguered near CHOR EL GHISMA after a quiet day, for which we were grateful.

That night in leaguer a motor cyclist and lorries were heard, apparently approaching from the direction of the enemy. We stood to and packed our bedding on our tanks ready to move if necessary. They passed close, though harmlessly, by, but some valuable sleep was lost. On the morning of the 30th, after opening leaguer, breakfast was disturbed by the news that German tanks were advancing upon us up the track from EL HASEIAT. We moved at once and took up a good hull down position facing south, still swallowing tea. A force of fifty German Mk. III's, most of them newly landed from Italy, attacked forthwith. They were, however, at a disadvantage for once, as our ridge was the shape of a horseshoe, and when they came in too near we were able to get them in the flank at close range. They endeavoured to send anti-tank guns round our left flank, but this was fortunately spotted and dealt with. Second-Lieutenant Slee and his crew were forced to evacuate their tank during this time, but were promptly rescued by Lieutenant King and brought back by another tank to the Regimental Navigator,[1] Second-Lieutenant Boyd.

---

[1] The Regimental Navigator, quite apart from navigating the Regiment from one point to another by day or night, had to plot the course of a battle, so that at any given moment, he knew exactly where the Regiment was. This, in battles moving to all points of the compass, sometimes a distance of yards and sometimes of miles, in country quite flat and with no landmarks whatever, was a task of immense difficulty. The Regiment was never on any occasion uncertain of its position, and always found its correct leaguer area.

RELIEVED BY 2ND ARMOURED BRIGADE

Then their artillery ranged on us, and their accurate fire, coupled with strong pressure from their tanks, forced us to move back to the next ridge. Our orders were to cover the withdrawal of the remaining armour and artillery, so it was necessary to hold each position to the last moment. We went back a Squadron at a time, and the last one to move suffered a desperate and difficult period till the next ridge was manned. On the second position the same process was gone through, and G Squadron were last to go. Captain Ling, as Squadron Leader, saw his Squadron away before attempting to depart himself, and as he was about to reverse off the slope his tank was hit and neither he nor his crew were ever traced. The news of his M.C., so well earned, came through that evening. The Germans, once again, did not press home their attack, having evidently achieved their object, and the afternoon was spent waiting for the battle to continue. But it did not, and we drew back into leaguer.

Our casualties were Captain Ling, Second-Lieutenant D'Arcy Francis, Corporal Langston, Lance-Corporal Hooper, Troopers Hill J., Hassall, Moss, and Stephens killed, and Second-Lieutenant Ades, Troopers Jones P., Ponting, and Reeves wounded.

The last day of the year was spent in open leaguer at the same place, and was marked by a Stuka raid on Brigade H.Q., the armoured command vehicle being punctured and set on fire by several pieces of bomb, one of which wounded General Lumsden, G.O.C. 1st Armoured Division, who had come on ahead of 2nd Armoured Brigade, newly arrived from England. The news that they were on their way up, strongly rumoured before, was now confirmed, and meant that we should be relieved, and the next day, the first of the New Year, we moved back into reserve east of Antelat. There we spent six days in peace and quiet, maintaining our vehicles and ourselves. Lord Apsley again came to see us, having come in his truck all the way from

2ND ROYAL GLOUCESTERSHIRE HUSSARS

the Delta to do so. This was the last occasion that he was able to visit us, for some time later, whilst flying home to England, he was killed.[1]

Thus ended the Regiment's part in the 1941 campaign, and we set off on the long march back to EL MRASSAS on the sea outside Tobruch. We travelled in the Echelon and ploughed our way across the desert in a blinding sandstorm.

As well as the decorations already mentioned, Lieutenant Milvain was awarded the M.C. He fought continuously through the campaign, and had indeed been fighting with 4th Armoured Brigade during the period the Regiment was refitting. Several times he rescued crews under the nose of the enemy, and on the Trigh Capuzzo, repaired his track, which had been shot off, while under heavy fire. Later, on two occasions, though his turret was penetrated and his tank useless as a fighting vehicle, he remained in action, thereby lending great moral support to his comrades. As this award did not come through for a very considerable time it can but be presumed that the recommendation was placed in a higher authorities' pending tray. Trooper Morse received the M.M. for consistently good gunnery. He knocked out nine tanks for certain and had other probables and many damaged. He never allowed heavy fire or overwhelming odds to upset his coolness and judgment, and did the maximum amount of damage with the minimum number of rounds.

We had suffered in casualties seven officers killed, six wounded, and nine missing; thirty-four other ranks killed, thirty-five wounded, forty-four missing, and thirty-four sick, a total of twenty-two officers and one hundred and forty-seven other ranks. But under immensely unfavourable conditions, outranged, outgunned, and outnumbered, though the battle at one time was practically lost, we had

[1] Lord Apsley served through the 1914–18 war, in which he won both the D.S.O. and M.C., with the Regiment. He remained a keen and enthusiastic Yeoman in the difficult years between the wars and lent not only great strength to the Regiment, but great help to old comrades.

HONEYS NEAR AGEDABIA

SQUADRON LEADER'S CONFERENCE NEAR SAUNNU

LT.-COL. BIRLEY REJOINS REGIMENT

assisted in driving the enemy the whole length of Cyrenaica, from the wire to the coast beyond Agedabia.

* * *

At El Mrassas we washed ourselves in a wintry sea and some were brave enough to bathe. We got our kit from the transport, put up tents and bivouacs, and made ourselves as comfortable as possible. We passed the time doing little or nothing, and generally took it easy. Squadron officers were the only people who were busy, and they were sorting out casualties, making returns, and writing letters to next-of-kin. Lieutenant-Colonel Birley returned, his arm mended but still in a sling. He had left the Delta before he was supposed to, and had got a lift to El Adem in a transport aeroplane. And never has a Commanding Officer shown such genuine pleasure at seeing his Regiment again. To be back in the desert, with his men, albeit many many miles from the battle, was to him like the first day of the holidays to a schoolboy. He radiated pride in the Regiment's achievements, but hid the great disappointment he felt at not having been with them. It was at this time that the award of his D.S.O. came through, and all ranks were pleased that his great courage at Bir el Gubi had been recognised.

Leave was now started, and half the Regiment left in high spirits for Alexandria and Cairo, to be followed in a few days by most of the remainder. The first party had to go in R.A.S.C. trucks across the desert to railhead, as Halfaya and Salum were still in enemy hands, but the second party were able to travel there by road and miss the trying journey with a bitter stormy night spent under a truck. The train to Mersa Matruh succeeded with great difficulty in averaging five miles an hour and during the last sixty minutes suffered from the most appalling attack of St. Vitus's Dance, throwing *quarante hommes* and their baggage from one end of the truck to the other with immense violence. Cairo and Alexandria were very full, but the Americans had not yet arrived, and prices were still only high, and not sky high, as they later became. It was possible, on three months' accumulated pay, to make up for the diet of bully beef, biscuits, and Tobruch water, and not very much of that, experienced during the campaign, and to stuff oneself with good things washed down with better things and to rest one's mind, if not improve it, with theatres, cinemas, night clubs, bathing, the Pyramids, and the Sphinx.

Meanwhile the Regiment, the framework of it, moved to BAQQUSH by the sea, a salubrious enough spot in summer, but at this time cursed by a continuous sandstorm blowing day and night at gale strength for the duration of the Regiment's stay. Here the leave parties rejoined, receiving a sharp reminder that life was still stern and still very full of sand.

At this moment Rommel started his counter-attack, which brought him to Gazala. When it became evident that it was making good progress, it was decided that 22nd Armoured Brigade should form a composite Regiment to be known as "Birley Force" under command of Lieutenant-Colonel Birley. There was very little indeed in front of Rommel to stop him, and "Birley Force" was placed as longstop at El Adem. Major White commanded 2 R.G.H Squadron, and their orders were that if Rommel reached El Adem they died to a man. Fortunately this was not required of them, and equally fortunately, when they were told to go forward to Msus to collect some tanks, General Norrie made them wait a day, for Msus and the tanks were already in German hands. When Rommel halted at Gazala, they returned to the Delta.

After ten days we moved back to Alexandria, to Sidi Bishr Camp, staying the night at El Daba. Here the whole Brigade was re-equipped, reformed, and strengthened by the addition of extra units, so that when we reached the desert again fresh training was needed. Sidi Bishr provided sleeping tents, mess tents, store tents, tents of every kind, running water, every modern convenience, modern in the Army sense, and easy access to Alexandria

"CRUSADER" AND "GRANT" TANKS

and the joys of civilisation and sophisticated night life. There were football and hockey matches against other units, sailing and golf, and the arrival of new tanks, Crusader tanks for G and H Squadrons, for F Squadron was to be equipped with Grants. This was a new tank to the British Army, and much larger and better armoured than anything we had seen before excepting the German Mk. III's and IV's, equipped with a 75-mm. gun and considered obsolete by the Americans in 1936. To receive these the Regiment moved to BENI YUSEF, near Cairo, where racing at Gezirêh was added to the gaiety of life. But serious work began. Tanks were put in order, as they always had to be when they were released by Ordnance, courses on driving and maintenance, wireless, gunnery, and the new Grant were run. Tactical exercises and lectures took place. Squadrons went to the neighbouring desert for training. The sergeants were invited to the officers' mess, with the result that it became considerably damaged, and on April 19th the Echelon left for the forward area, the tanks following by train and transporter. On April 28th the whole Regiment was in camp, thirty miles west of Capuzzo, ready for final training and firing, and, with the rest of 22nd Armoured Brigade, came under command of 1st Armoured Division.

* * *

We settled down to desert existence again some miles south of BIR ES SUFAN. It was the same inhospitable desert and it had not changed in our absence—flat as far as the eye could see, stony and covered in scrub, and not even the map could find a name for our camp. But the weather was warmer this time, and we experienced delightful days of moderate temperature, forerunners of boiling heat to come. No sooner had we arrived than the desert performed a miracle, and became covered in green grass, studded with thousands of tiny mauve flowers. But Nature could not stand it, and on second thoughts began to withdraw, and in a few days had vanished. Its place, however,

2ND ROYAL GLOUCESTERSHIRE HUSSARS

was taken by troops and by tanks, by trucks and by guns, by ambulances and dressing stations, dumps and stores, and even by one or two of the new and secret 6-pounder guns that, with the Grant tanks, were to give the Germans the shock of their lives. So crowded did the scene become that it was difficult to spot one's own unit from any distance, and impossible to keep a straight course on a compass bearing. Driving in the dark became a nightmare, and the new rule that men should sleep twenty yards from their vehicles, in case of fire from lighted cigarettes, added a fresh hazard to life in the forward area.

Training commenced, and each Squadron went south into the "blue" to fire their guns, and stayed two nights. F Squadron were delayed for a day by a sandstorm, which smote them the evening they arrived at the range. It could be seen approaching across the desert, at first a "black cloud the size of a man's hand," and steadily growing till it resembled a great mountain towering many hundreds of feet into the air. It gave time, however, for bedding and kit to be pushed hurriedly under tank sheets, and quick preparations to be made before it finally enveloped the camp. The 75-mm. was found to be very accurate and made a most satisfying bang, and it fired high explosive as well as armour piercing shot. For high explosive fire it was necessary to range on the target, and it was decided that the 2nd in command of the Squadron should find the range and give it out on the wireless. This worked well once a method of describing whole turns and fractions of turns of the elevating wheel had been evolved. The formula, however, had not been perfected when a demonstration was given, and only the 2nd in command's rounds reached the target area, the other eleven tanks all falling short. But so much smoke and sand were thrown up by the bursting shells that none of the Generals present was any the wiser, and they expressed great satisfaction at what they had seen.

There followed something quite new in training—

TRAINING WITH "THE BOX"

training with "the Box." The Box consisted of a Battery of 107th Royal Horse Artillery (the South Notts Hussars), a Reconnaissance Company of Northumberland Fusiliers, and a troop of anti-tank guns. In theory, the Box was to be an immovable strong point set down when necessary, with the armour kept ready to counter attack, and what enemy would by-pass an immovable strong point supported by tanks? In practice, Boxes were in danger of facing the wrong way or locking the tanks up inside their confines, thus preventing any manoeuvring, or of being just overrun. They gave the enemy some trouble, but not enough, with the exception of the Guards' Box at Knightsbridge, which, with the help of the Armoured Brigades, freed from their own shattered Boxes, was a great stumbling block to the Germans, and they were only withdrawn when the positions elsewhere became untenable. Training with the Box was very muddling and made more difficult by sandstorms, and nobody really understood it till the Regiment gave a demonstration left flank attack against the Box. We were allowed to fire smoke and the "battlefield" looked most realistic, a final touch being added by Captain Gordon-Creed scoring a direct hit on a truck and frightening its crew out of their lives.

Before moving up to our battle position, which was to be done by means of an exercise, F Squadron gave a demonstration shoot for the Duke of Gloucester. Piles of barrels were put up as targets and a derelict German Mk. II tank was towed into position. The range selected was such that there was no chance of anything being left of the barrels, and the tank was, in fact, well riddled and the rubber tyres caught fire. H.R.H., however, insisted that the inside had been soaked in petrol.

The next few days were spent packing up, and making final arrangements to go forward and putting lorry hoods on the Grants, for the enemy were to be kept in ignorance of their presence, always providing they had not been told about them by their agents in the Delta or caught a glimpse of them lumbering about the desert on training. General Lumsden, G.O.C. 1st Armoured Division, came to see us and spoke to every officer in the Brigade individually, a feat rarely performed by a Divisional Commander in such circumstances and at that time.

We moved off on May 16th and the exercise on the journey defied even the most acute military mind. It was remarkable, however, for General Lumsden appearing in the most unexpected places in an armoured car, and thereby finding people not exercising very happily, and for his anger at finding F Squadron in echelon formation instead of tank formation. But as they were camouflaged as trucks and were meant to represent an echelon the General came off second best!

That evening the Brigade reached its position at NADURET EL GHESCEUASC and faced north with 2 R.G.H. on the right. Our first task was to dig in all soft vehicles and, as this was a particularly tough piece of desert, it took some time to get the bonnet of a three-tonner below ground level. Crews maintained their tanks, cleaned their ammunition, and got ready to move at short notice. It was known that Eighth Army was not quite prepared, but it was not known how ready were Rommel and his Afrika Corps, and every time a dispatch rider—there was wireless silence—was seen to leave the Orderly Room truck it was thought that he carried orders to line up to receive them. Officers and tank commanders spent the time reconnoitring every possible route by which they might come so that they would know, or think they knew, where they were when they met them. After ten days, during which the tension had eased considerably, we were suddenly, and at an hour's notice, told to move and take up a position to cover gaps in the minefield just south of BIR EL HARMAT. During the afternoon we moved through the 2nd Armoured Brigade, who were the other half of 1st Armoured Division, and came into Brigade reserve, facing south, with thirty-six

FORT CAPUZZO, 1942

B ECHELON MOVING UP ALONG THE COAST ROAD

MINEFIELDS

officers, five hundred and sixty-three other ranks, forty-eight tanks, scout cars, and a complete Echelon, while the 3rd and 4th County of London Yeomanry faced north-west.

It was considered that the Germans might attack in one or more of three ways. In the north through the minefield by Gazala and then east along the coast road to Tobruch; in the middle through the minefield, and then north-east to Tobruch; or round the south end of the minefield and north-east to Tobruch. This was the first time we had experienced minefields in the desert, though Tobruch had been protected by them the winter before. We had had no training in mines, and did not know how to cope with them, so we were delighted to find the whole danger area surrounded by wire with "Mines" written on our side and "Minen" on the other. But the echelon experienced trouble and suffered casualties from enemy mines left outside Tobruch and never cleared away. The minefield stretched from the sea at Gazala south to Bir Hacheim, where the fighting French were placed; and they were destined in the next two weeks to fight one of the fiercest battles in the annals of French history. Next, to the north, came 7th Armoured Division with 4th Armoured Brigade, then 1st Armoured Division with 22nd Armoured Brigade by the minefield, and 2nd Armoured Brigade just east of them in reserve; then the Guards' Box at Knightsbridge and beyond them 50th Division and an Army Tank Brigade. Finally the South African Division formed the Gazala Box, and South African Armoured cars and 7th Motor Brigade were on the German side of the minefield patrolling. Second-Lieutenant Knight-Bruce had been sent to the 50th Division to act as *liaison* officer, but the course of the battle prevented him performing this duty.[1] It was thought that

---

[1] Second-Lieutenant Knight-Bruce was, however, given a troop of Crusaders and told to protect H.Q., and he was able to do valuable patrols and knock out several German tanks before being captured with the rest of the Box. At the Italian Armistice he escaped, and during four months he covered five hundred miles through the mountains of Italy and passed safely through Eighth Army lines in December 1943.

the most probable German approach was at Gazala, so 3rd and 4th County of London Yeomanry were faced north-west to be able to go at once to assist in that direction. 2 R.G.H. were faced south to back up 4th Armoured Brigade should they be attacked, and were it north or south the whole Brigade would eventually join up wherever the crisis occurred. In the unlikely event of a break through the middle of the minefield we merely turned to face it. Why the Higher Command seemed to favour a German attack in the north, and why they appeared to think the enemy would take on a strongly defended minefield instead of employing the classic desert tactic of coming round the south end of the line, was never explained. Rommel, though he did attack at Gazala, preferred the line of least resistance, coupled with the advantage of an outflanking movement, and made his main effort with his armour round Bir Hacheim.

Just before dark the Colonel vouchsafed to Squadron Leaders the information that 15th and 21st Panzer Divisions had left their positions by the sea and were at large somewhere on the other side of the minefield. We finished our evening "brew up" and prepared to go to bed, in open leaguer formation, with a sinking feeling in our stomachs for, though there was no information for the rank and file, the atmosphere was tense, and gave the suggestion that the first ball was about to be bowled and we might well catch it on the shins in the morning. Nor was this impression lessened after dark. Verey lights began, and continued, to go up over the minefield to the south of us. A report came in of twenty Italian tanks protecting a gapping party. At midnight they had swelled to ninety German tanks. It was ominously quiet, and only the noise of a wireless set being put into one of the Grants disturbed the stillness, and the Verey lights the darkness. We did not sleep so calmly as we had done before Bir el Gubi; we knew what to expect this time.

*   *   *

GERMAN TANKS APPROACHING

By first light nothing further had transpired and we did P.T. and "brewed up." Presumably, as the enemy had not appeared at dawn, the customary time, he had decided to put it off for a day. But as we were finishing breakfast Squadron Leaders were summoned by the Colonel to the Orderly Room truck; Sergeant Bywater, on the telephone, gave the order for camouflage hoods to be taken off, for crews to mount and to be ready to go into battle immediately. Shells began falling a short way to the south and then almost amongst us. Squadron Leaders ran back and shouted to their assembled Troop Leaders to mount, form line, and advance towards 4th Armoured Brigade and our own Box, who were heavily engaged with German tanks. We had barely got moving before tanks were seen approaching through the dust and haze and H Squadron, who were in the centre, were ordered to send a patrol forward to discover if it was 4th Armoured Brigade withdrawing or the Panzer Divisions advancing. Second-Lieutenant Proctor, with his Troop, went forward and almost immediately had his tank knocked out. He jumped to the ground and ran towards his Troop Sergeant's tank to send a message, but was seriously wounded in the stomach and side by a high explosive shell. Sergeant A'Bear, without hesitation and under heavy fire, went to his assistance and carried him to his own tank. Having sent the message, he drove him out of the danger zone and back to a dressing station. His tank, during this time, received nine direct hits. For this action, which saved his Troop Leader's life, Sergeant A'Bear received the M.M. Meanwhile the Regiment having just had time to shake out, had opened fire, there being no doubt that the approaching tanks were Germans. Nevertheless "cease fire" was given forthwith over the air, and the information that it was 4th Armoured Brigade coming back. Scant notice, however, was taken of this order, which indeed was only passed over the regimental frequency as it had come from Brigade, since there was no tank in view that resembled a

British one, nor would 4th Armoured Brigade have opened fire on us. But it did put us off for a moment, and gave the sixty odd German tanks a chance of gaining a little ground before the Grants settled down to make use of the long range of their 75 mm. guns. It was now obvious that 7th Armoured Division and our own Box had been over-run and it was our job to stop the enemy till the 3rd and 4th County of London Yeomanry could turn round and other help could be sent. We did not know that sixty other German tanks had made a wider sweep and were steaming to the east of us, drawing off any assistance from our reserves. No satisfactory explanation was ever given as to why no information reached the troops concerned of the enemy attack. The Commanding Officer was informed that the two Panzer Divisions had moved from their original positions, but nothing further came through. It was subsequently discovered that the South African Armoured cars had run parallel with the enemy during their move south, had kept them under close observation, and had reported at frequent intervals their every move. That their information reached the appropriate H.Q. there can be no doubt, as their signals were acknowledged, and it has been inferred that the H.Q. replied, telling the South Africans to think again, as it could not be the Afrika Corps, though who else it could have been it is difficult to imagine. At any rate, no apparent notice was taken of this vital information, and, as far as we were concerned, it remained in the Staff's pending tray.

Whether the Germans knew about the Grant tank has never been settled, but at all events they concentrated their whole strength against F Squadron, who were on the right. A tremendous battle ensued, and it did not die down until every Grant, except one, had either been knocked out or had run out of ammunition and was so badly damaged that it could not have gone on fighting had it had any left. Almost at the beginning the Squadron Leader, Major

DEVASTATING LOSSES IN F SQUADRON

King, had his track knocked off,[1] and the wireless set of Captain Pitman (the 2nd in command) was put out of action. Only four tanks got away from the first "stand," and they only moved when the enemy were within six hundred yards. Fire of every kind was intense and the dust and smoke of high explosive made it immensely difficult to follow what was happening. Tanks were burning on every side, and the thick black pall of smoke caused by the fires added to the confusion. No orders could be given and it was impossible to see signals, so every crew fought its own battle. Armour piercing shells slammed against the front plate, knocking equipment and showers of paint to the floor inside. But the front armour of the Grant was good and withstood the enemy fire. Two tanks stood again just in front of the 3rd County of London Yeomanry. And not till their ammunition was finished, and the enemy again within six hundred yards, did they back away, experiencing agonising minutes as they turned round, exposing their broadside, and slowly crawl off till they were out of range. Of the four tanks that survived, three were so badly damaged that it was necessary to transport them from the field, and one had received no less than fourteen direct hits.

Though it was never known what number of enemy tanks were destroyed, many were seen immovable on the battlefield, and they suffered a considerable set-back. But this was achieved at the cost of devastating losses in F Squadron. Of the twenty-eight casualties Lieutenant Ades, Sergeant Byard, Corporal Chamberlain, and Troopers Buxton, Sergeant and Parry were killed; Troopers Boughton, Jones, and Morse were wounded; and Sergeant Greaves, Corporals Astley, Rodway F., and Troopers Amos, Bell, Bridle, Burry, Davison, Jewell, Pearce, Pavitt, Pike, Solovitch, Wilks, Wilkins, Harvey, Tovey, and Woods were

---

[1] He and his crew were rescued by the Crusader that had been allotted to him as a spare rear link. The Grants, having American wireless sets, were on a separate frequency.

2ND ROYAL GLOUCESTERSHIRE HUSSARS

taken prisoner. Trooper Webb was missing and later reported killed. Of the prisoners, Corporal Rodway, Troopers Amos, Bell, Davison, and Bridle were wounded, while Trooper Woods managed to escape that night and make his way back to our lines, arriving in the morning exhausted by hunger and thirst; Second-Lieutenant Summerell had his tank hit and his first and second driver wounded. Ordering his gunner to continue firing, he climbed down to the driving compartment and, though in the thick of battle, dressed the two men's wounds before driving the tank out of danger himself. For his coolness during a period in which the risk to himself was very great he received the M.C. Corporal Yool had his tank set on fire and, when every effort to put out the flames had failed, ordered his crew to bale out. When some way from the tank he realised that his 75-mm. gunner was still in it, wounded. Accompanied by Corporal Poole he went back. Both of them, under very heavy fire indeed, with difficulty got the gunner out and carried him to safety. For running great personal risk to rescue a comrade Corporal Poole received the M.M. Corporal Yool, for this act coupled with another still to be recounted, was awarded the D.C.M.

Trooper Bridle, of F Squadron, gives the following description of this action—

May 27th, 1942, at BIR HARMAT, near BIR HACHEIM, you know yourself how suddenly we got the news of the German attack and how we had to rush around closing doors, throwing the wagon covers off, and getting the kit aboard. Well, I must say, everybody moved very quickly, and in next-to-no-time we were all set. We were all pretty calm, and I shall always remember Johnnie Chamberlain, for while high explosive was dropping, though it was well out on the flank, and not worrying us, he sat on the tank and painted the name on it. Mr. Ades came rushing back and we all mounted and I started up. I kept an eagle eye out

SALUM AND THE ESCARPMENT

SALUM FROM HALF-WAY UP THE ESCARPMENT

To face page 58

TPR. BRIDLE'S ACCOUNT OF ACTION

of the periscope and watched them top the hill in front of us. Yes, there was no mistaking them, that long line coming straight at us. I counted them, and they were near on sixty, though I couldn't see their farthermost flank, and I wondered when we were going to open up, and it wasn't till they opened up on us that we returned fire. I should think that we were between twelve or fifteen hundred yards away. All the crew were very steady, and we had all guns blazing, including the machine guns. The electric solenoid on the 75-mm. broke, and I had to use a hammer on the hand trigger as the pressure was too great for the gunner, who was Charlie Solovitch. He said he got four tanks, but I cannot say as to that, though I did see quite a few blazing merrily. They came on and on, and Mr. Ades kept me weaving around, though for no great distance. During this time, I had not seen any tanks of ours up as far as we were, though of course they were, but everything was going pretty quick. I did think at the time that we were in too close and would have been better if we had retired, which the rest of the Squadron had been doing, though I wasn't aware of it at the time, and I was all set for the order to wheel around. Up to that time no serious damage was done to us, but they were in close then, eight hundred yards, and nearly up to us on the flanks, and just our troop, though I was unaware that the rest of the Squadron had retired, and so obviously they concentrated on us, and we had four direct hits in less than a minute. The first shattered a track and I felt it go, almost instantaneously.

Another came in through the final drives, wounding the 75-mm. gunner and must have just missed me; the third came clean in through the side door, just missing the high explosive box and killing Buxton, the loader, and Corporal Chamberlain. It must have been a powerful shot, for it was a very neat hole and wasn't even burred. The fourth shot must have gone straight into the engine, for almost immediately the flames roared through on both sides of the turret and Mr. Ades shouted to bale out. I asked Solovitch if Buxton was dead, though I saw him drop myself, and he said he was definitely killed, so I told him to get out, and he crossed over me and straight into the turret and out the far side. I went out last and took a quick glance at Johnnie Chamberlain; there was no doubt whatsoever, he was definitely killed. I went out the side door, and Mr. Ades was waiting there. He was very confident, and said, "Don't worry, lad, we'll get out of this yet." As soon as we were out, I had a quick bearing of what was going on. Sergeant Byard's tank was on the left flank, and a little behind us; it was also a raging inferno. Just having baled out, Sergeant Byard, Corporal Pavitt, Troopers Bell, Frank Rodway, and Bill Harvey were running towards Sergeant Greaves's tank, which was behind us again. He was obviously prepared to get us out quickly, and had half turned the tank when we all piled on the back. Well, we all breathed again. But only for a short while. Just as Trooper Amos was changing into fourth gear the tank got a direct hit in the engine and instantly roared into flames. We all fell, or got knocked off the tank. Frank Rodway was very badly wounded in about seven places. Trooper Bell got wounded in the mouth and Davison got badly hit in his hand. The crew of Sergeant Greaves did not have an earthly. Sergeant Greaves was not wounded, but only Trooper D. Williams and Trooper C. Amos got out, and only just. Both were very badly burnt.

Trooper Amos had a very narrow escape, he pulled himself up out of the side hatch, and even now I can see his muscles straining, getting his stomach on the top of the hatch, he rolled himself off the side and landed head over heels on the ground, exhausted. So for a while, to get a breather, we all stood beside the tank, though there were a lot of machine guns blazing away. Mr. Ades was still game, though we were in an impossible position; our tanks were in the distance and only at one time did we have

ACCOUNT OF ACTION

any hopes—a Cruiser tank, wheeling around, seemed to be coming towards us, but at the least it was a good eight hundred or thousand yards away, and seeing how hopeless it was it turned around and retired. But Mr. Ades suggested that those who could, and wanted to, should make a run for it, at least to try and hide in a dug-out until the boys came in again; to try to get right away would have been suicide, as it was proved. The German tanks were about four or five hundred yards in front of us and already past on the flanks. But nevertheless he went, telling us to run at intervals, so as not to bunch together. Corporal Pavitt was just running off, and I was going to follow, although my leg was very stiff through a small wound which had tightened the muscles, but I didn't run, for Mr. Ades hadn't gone forty yards before he was hit by a belt of explosive bullets. Corporal Pavitt went up to him and turned him over; he was between us and Mr. Ades and didn't have far to go, but it was useless, and he turned back to us. During this time there was a constant flow of machine gun bullets, and we had to be extremely careful. By this time the Germans were up to us, and one of their tank officers told us to put our hands up and walk towards their rear. Just then our own 25's opened up and we had to contend with them, and believe me, they were shooting well. During all this time Sergeant Greaves was certainly a stone wall, always very cool he devoted himself to helping those badly wounded boys and took no consideration for himself. He suggested that we should get into some cover, as, for one thing, the tank was liable to blow up at any time as one had already, and as you know, they certainly do go up with forty rounds of high explosive. So we moved off, and only just in time. As it was, Sergeant Byard got killed for not moving off soon enough. We looked back as it went off and saw Sergeant Byard stop in his tracks and drop. I believe it was Trooper Bell who went back to him, but it was no good. So we went on, and still our high explosive was dropping, and then I suddenly spotted a dug-out that had been used for driving a wagon into. So we all took cover in this.

During this time the boys had suffered a lot with their burns and wounds, and we had a smoke. Wilkins was the only one who had any cigarettes out of the lot of us, though we left hundreds behind. Well, shortly afterwards, a German infantryman poked his head over the dug-out and seeing the state most of us were in, went and fetched a doctor, and I must say he gave us every consideration, and even while he dressed us he made a German wait who was stretched out on a tank. From there, Corporal Rodway and Troopers Amos and Wilkins and myself went in an ambulance, myself more or less to look after them. From there to Derna, and after a couple of days on a hospital boat to Italy. I was lucky, as for the seriousness of my wounds I shouldn't have gone, but perhaps it was the way I was dressed, and perhaps I have Sergeant Greaves to thank for that. But the farther we went back, the worse things seemed to get. Life as a prisoner was not too rosy and I try to forget all these things, but at times I don't think I will, and I know I shall never forget that grand bunch of boys who fought and died with us, generally with the odds against us, but always with that grand spirit.

During this time G and H Squadrons had opened fire, but the range was too great for their 2-pounders to be effective. G Squadron was ordered to help F Squadron, but as they were crossing over behind R.H.Q. the order for the Regiment to retire to a position just in front of the Knightsbridge Box was received. Here we remained for a short while watching 6-pounders in action for the first time from the Box, and firing a few rounds ourselves. Lieutenant Peel and his Troop, who were out in front of the Regiment observing some tanks of unknown nationality, had his own tank hit and his gunner wounded, and was unable to pick up his troop sergeant and his crew when

REGIMENT'S SEVERE CASUALTIES

their tank shed a track. Three of the crew—Sergeant Houghton, Troopers Dean and Merchant-Locke—were captured and the operator, Trooper Mackrell, was killed. We now withdrew behind the Box to replenish, and remained some time below a ridge in comparative safety. The enemy never in fact got over this ridge as they found the anti-tank weapons of the Knightsbridge Box too powerful for them. In the evening the Regiment moved a short distance to take on, and repel, an enemy attack with twenty-five Mk. III's and IV's coming from the west, and at last light we moved into leaguer very tired and weary, realising that first light was only three or four hours away. During the morning, the Echelon, now commanded by Major Jerden, had had its share of the German attack. Another enemy column, travelling far round the British flank with the intention of cutting the road east of Tobruch, had assailed them unannounced south of El Adem. However they withdrew in good order with no damage, though for a time under considerable shell fire. In addition to the casualties mentioned Corporal Cook and Troopers Kermarec, Lockwood, Marshall, Maynard, and Prosser were wounded; Troopers Rogers, Wilson, and Furnivall taken prisoner; Trooper Cook T. C. was also captured and died of exhaustion a week after, while Corporal Griffiths, though made a prisoner, succeeded in rejoining our lines three days later. These forty-three casualties were, next to the battle of Bir el Gubi, the severest blow the Regiment suffered, but it had very materially assisted in stopping the enemy onslaught, aimed at the immediate capture of Tobruch, and the subsequent and rapid destruction of Eighth Army.

The following day the Regiment, less F Squadron, which had ceased to exist, barring one tank, remained at BIR BELLEFAA, south of the Knightsbridge Box, and, as the enemy were expected to break through in an easterly direction north of Bir Bellefaa, spent the night as a thin, and wakeful, red line. In the morning we watched a large

2ND ROYAL GLOUCESTERSHIRE HUSSARS

German concentration, but were shortly moved south-west to support 2nd Armoured Brigade and 3rd County of London Yeomanry, who were heavily engaged. G Squadron went to help 3rd County of London Yeomanry and had a battle lasting about one and a half hours, during which Lieutenant Peel had his tank knocked out. H Squadron with R.H.Q. were sent to intercept an enemy column advancing from Bir el Harmat, and during their engagement Second-Lieutenant Meade's troop got right in amongst the Germans. Two of his tanks got back, but Sergeant Pearson went clean through the position and, after wandering about in the enemy lines for an hour or two, met some Matildas and accompanied them to 50th Division Box. He and his crew, Corporal Woods and Trooper Ryalls, were captured when 50th Division were over-run. The next morning, the 30th, the Regiment went to help 4th and 7th Armoured Brigades in an attack on Bir el Harmat. This was made nine Regiments up, and, as it was prepared in full view of the enemy, was not successful, though some anti-tank guns were destroyed. In the afternoon we lined up to receive the expected counter-attack, which did not, however, materialise. Two G Squadron troops went to the 9th Lancers for an attack in the evening, but returned to leaguer with the Regiment. During the day 2nd Lieutenant Summerell drove his scout car over a mine and broke an ear drum, and Trooper Reeves was also wounded. By now everyone was very tired, for there was seldom more than four hours' sleep and the heat was most trying. By the time the Regiment had withdrawn into leaguer at night and filled up from A.1 Echelon it was midnight and first light broke at about 4 a.m. So it was a relief for some when a composite Squadron was formed under Major King. This joined the 3rd County of London Yeomanry.

The remainder went back to A.1 Echelon, though some returned to B Echelon, who were below the escarpment between El Adem and Tobruch. They were leaguered on a

GRANT TANK NEAR KNIGHTSBRIDGE

DESERT DUST

A BRIGHT MOON AND TRYING NIGHTS

minefield left from the campaign before, and driving about the area was fraught with danger. Several trucks blew up, including Regimental Sergeant-major Lee's 15 cwt., and casualties were sustained.

At night—there was a bright moon—enemy raiders, returning from sorties to Alexandria and elsewhere along the coast, bombed and machine-gunned the leaguer. Though no damage was done, it reduced sleep to a minimum, and was most wearing to the nerves. Nothing is more trying than to hear the drone of planes and the whistle of bombs and to see tracer bullets gliding towards one and, with no protection—for the desert was too rocky to dig slit trenches—to be forced merely to lie flat on one's stomach and be unable to retaliate.

Meantime the composite Squadron, under command of 3rd County of London Yeomanry, were ordered to stand by for an infantry attack, but nothing happened, though Corporal Walters[1] and Troopers Gothard and Hunt, were wounded, and on the following day two patrols, under Captain Gordon-Creed and Second-Lieutenant Jeffery, were sent forward to test some enemy tanks on a ridge at BIR EL ASLAGH. They were found to be derelict, but there were anti-tank guns amongst them. Sergeant Ogden's tank was hit, Troopers Hall and Novell were killed, and Trooper Oxborough and Sergeant Ogden were wounded, but Sergeant Ogden got his tank back with difficulty and reported his information to his Squadron Leader, refusing to be evacuated or have his wound dressed till he had done so. For this he received the M.M. Sergeant Allies and Sergeant Brackenbury[2] were also awarded the M.M. They and their Squadron fitters had worked during these trying days with immense energy, usually under heavy fire, and had succeeded in keeping most of their damaged or overworked tanks on the road. On the next day, June 2nd,

---

[1] Corporal Walters died of his wounds later.
[2] Sergeant Brackenbury's award also covered his work on July column.

the composite Squadron came back, and the Regiment moved to Rear Brigade to refit and receive badly needed reinforcements.

June 2nd to 4th were spent a short distance east of Bir Bellefaa. We took over two Squadrons of Honeys and one of Grants from the 4th Hussars, and met Major Knight again, who had been with the Regiment as Adjutant and a Squadron Leader from before the War till we went abroad, when he joined his own Regiment in the Middle East. Reinforcements arrived from the Tank Reinforcement Squadron, and they were quickly sorted out and put into crews. F Squadron however, did not receive enough and were not complete till a few hours before the next battle. Major White, who had been commanding H Squadron, went back to B Echelon and was subsequently evacuated to hospital, and Captain Taylor, 2nd in command of B Echelon, came up and took over from him. The desert in the neighbourhood was littered with enemy equipment, for this time we had succeeded in holding the battlefield and preventing the Germans from evacuating their destroyed vehicles. And there were a great many Mk. III's and IV's which the Royal Engineers were busy blowing up—proof that in the 6-pounder anti-tank gun and the Grant we at last could match the Germans in fire power. It was said that no fewer than three hundred tanks had been knocked out, but this information was taken with a pinch of salt, usually necessary where reports of enemy casualties were concerned.

The position at this moment appeared to be that the enemy had decided that we were too much for him and was withdrawing. He was either wedged in a precarious position between Eighth Army and the minefield, struggling to get through his few gaps, or else bogged down on the minefield. It was felt by everyone that a quick follow up and, in particular, an armoured sortie round the minefield and their flank would have put them in such straits that the days of the Afrika Corps might have been numbered. We

REFORMING FOR ATTACK JUNE 5th

were, of course, pretty groggy ourselves and in dire need of reforming, but sitting doing nothing, and as far as pressing home our advantage was concerned we were doing nothing for the best part of a week, and giving Rommel every opportunity of extricating himself, did not suit our mood. And so quick was Rommel to seize this respite that he even gave up extricating himself, and, turning round, brought up everything he had to be ready on June 5th to give Eighth Army a blow from which it did not recover till it stood at El Alamein. By the time we were ready on June 4th, gunfire, which had been distant to the west of us, was creeping nearer, and we began to realise that our chance was slipping and had perhaps gone. That evening, with thirty-two Honeys and twelve Grants, we moved into position with the 4th County of London Yeomanry just east of Bir el Harmat.

Orders for an attack the next day were given out just before we close leaguered and were interrupted by a bombing attack, the weight of which fell on troops a little farther forward. The enemy, we were told, was esconced on two ridges at Bir el Aslagh. A preliminary bombardment commencing at 3 a.m. was to be followed by the taking of the first ridge by the Indians, who would also capture all the anti-tank guns thereon. This would leave the way perfectly clear for 22nd Armoured Brigade to rush the second ridge, turn north and then east again, thus clearing the enemy from his only hold on a gap in the minefield. This meant a frontal attack by armour on a defended position, and an attack of this kind by cavalry tanks, though even then considered part of their role, is one of the surest methods of suicide that exists, and the plan, with memories of similar attacks in the past in our minds, did not tend to raise our spirits. We went into close leaguer, and at midnight F Squadron's remaining reinforcements arrived and had to be put into crews. This took some considerable time, and at 3 a.m. the barrage, the biggest employed up to that time, started. The guns were not far from the leaguer and further sleep was impossible, and many that night had only an hour or two.

At the first glimmer of dawn on June 5th we moved a short distance to our forming up place, and awaited the success signal from the Indians. This was not forthcoming at the expected time, so our attack was put off for a quarter of an hour. Then it did come, and we set off at our best pace into the haze and mirage. We passed through the Indians on the first ridge, but saw no signs of any Germans, dead or alive, and no captured anti-tank guns. These, the moment an attack was suspected, and, it seems, contrary to the appreciation of the Higher Command, the Germans had thoughtfully withdrawn to the second ridge, where they proposed to stand and take on our armour. We lumbered on up the long gradual slope, the leading tanks practically blinding those following with their trails of dust, and when we were about half way the enemy opened fire. He had made good use of the few days' grace he had been allowed, and had brought up every gun he could lay his hands on. With these, and the tanks he had been able to collect, he laid about us. He was drawn up in a semicircle and let us get just to the mouth of it, and his fire, of every calibre, poured upon us from in front and from both sides. We were saved from complete disaster by the fact that he began his battle at long range, the fact that he was firing into the rising sun and the mirage, and the fact that his fire from field guns, up to 150-mm., was so intense that he obliterated us in smoke and dust. But we could see nothing either, and came to a standstill, not only because we could see no targets to shoot at, but also because the atmosphere was such that it became impossible to keep visual contact amongst ourselves. We stayed in this position for a while, weaving about and watching high explosive shells bursting and throwing up great yellow and black plumes, and listened to the double bark of their explosions. Sometimes one would crash against the outside of a tank, clanging on the armour

FAILURE TO CLOSE MINEFIELD GAP

plating, and shake up the sweating crew inside. One such knocked off Major Taylor's track, and Trooper Godfrey was shot in the head and killed as he baled out, while Corporal Mizon was wounded in the knee. Captain Maunsell, 2nd in command of H Squadron, sensing rather than seeing that something was wrong, came across and, dismounting under this intense fire, assisted in getting the crew into his tank. He got them safely back and, for his hazardous work performed at great personal danger, he was awarded the M.C. Corporal Yool's tank during this time developed engine trouble, and he managed to get it into a disused vehicle pit. Refusing his Squadron Leader's offer to come out and pick up himself and his crew, under very heavy fire, he repaired it and brought it back safely. This, coupled with his action at Bir el Harmat previously mentioned, earned him the D.C.M.

The Regiment now rallied and withdrew a little and lined up to face west. We were placed only just in front of our anti-tank guns and 25-pounders and during the afternoon two attacks of about twenty German tanks were beaten off. Otherwise, for most of the time, we sat sweltering in our tanks, quenching our thirst with hot water from our water bottles, while the desire to fall asleep was countered by bursting shells. At about 4 p.m. F Squadron were sent to the right flank to assist some Matildas, and Major King's tank was set on fire. He and his crew got out and were taken to safety by Second-Lieutenant Slee. This officer was then sent slightly forward of the Regiment to range on the enemy to enable the Grants to bring down high explosive fire, but so quick and accurate was the reply that the attempt was abandoned. In the evening a serious attack seemed about to be launched on the 3rd County of London Yeomanry on our left, and F Squadron was sent to help them. It failed, however, properly to materialise, though two Mk. IV's were hit and set on fire at long range. As dusk fell we were ordered to withdraw to go into leaguer, and we left the battlefield, dotted with burning vehicles, under a twilit sky bright with floating Verey lights and tracer bullets. We finally leaguered at 12.30 a.m. close to what was strongly suspected to be a German column that had been running parallel to us for some time. We had heard the faint rumbling of tanks and vehicles and seen mysterious Verey lights keeping up with us, and had passed through an Indian Brigade which was later that night overrun by German tanks. Considering what might and, we felt, should have happened, our casualties were remarkably light. As well as those mentioned we lost Lieutenant Peel, a prisoner, and Troopers Crane, Rowarth, Nash, and Tomlins wounded.

We opened leaguer the next morning and had just started breakfast when, in the clearing mist, we saw our German column of the night before, well equipped with guns, a few thousand yards from us. These opened fire on our own artillery behind us, and they replied, and we found ourselves in the position of a tennis net. Fortunately, the contestants were keeping their shots well up and we were able to gobble our meal and move away without one being put into it. We formed up with 3rd County of London Yeomanry in front of the Guards' Box and watched some twenty-five German tanks while their guns shelled us, knocking out two Grants and one Honey. As they did not move we advanced east to conform with 3rd County of London Yeomanry and were very heavily shelled from the south-east by 88-mm. guns; 3rd County of London Yeomanry turned north into a valley near Bir Bellefaa and we did the same. During this move the Colonel's tank became somewhat separated and was hit by a shell from a battery of 88's. Major Taylor was the first to see his tank stationary and a figure on the ground waving. He went quickly across and found the Colonel who, in spite of having both legs almost shot off at the knee, had got himself out of his tank to attract assistance. His driver,

CAPTAIN
M. G. LING, M.C.

MAJOR
W. A. B. TREVOR, D.S.O.

LIEUTENANT COLONEL
N. A. BIRLEY, D.S.O.

MAJOR REINHOLD

To face page 71

THE REGIMENT LOSES ITS COLONEL

Corporal Dickinson, was badly wounded in the face and shoulder, and Captain Muir, the Adjutant, and Corporal Froggatt, his operator, had been killed instantaneously by the shell which had passed straight through the tank as if through matchboard. Major Taylor and Trooper Docherty, his gunner, dismounted, and got the Colonel and Corporal Dickinson on to the front of their tank, and with Trooper Docherty riding on the outside under heavy fire to prevent them falling off, brought them to some gunners a short distance away. There they were put into a 15 cwt. truck and taken to a dressing station. Corporal Dickinson survived and recovered, but Lieutenant-Colonel Birley died at the dressing station from loss of blood and shock. Trooper Docherty was awarded the M.M. for his part in this action.

This was a profound and shattering blow to the Regiment; a blow not only because the Colonel had been killed, but because Charles Birley had been killed. From the moment he came to us in April, 1940, he had worked tirelessly with one end and one end only in view—to get the Regiment into battle as soon as possible in such a state of material and moral efficiency that would enable it to fight on equal terms with any unit with which it came into the line. And the battles that it had fought and the battle that it was fighting at the moment of his death proved not only to him, but to those who fought alongside, that his task and his ambition had been amply fulfilled. Nor was this task easy. He found us unequipped and, therefore, only trained in the simplest military matters, and we had for many months to be ready, first and foremost, to repel the expected invasion, which forced training, pure and simple, to become a secondary role. During the long months of preparation before the Regiment went abroad, he found it most difficult, if not impossible, to fathom, or indeed to cope with, the Yeomanry spirit and their lighthearted and friendly way of doing things. Their idea of military life and discipline

2ND ROYAL GLOUCESTERSHIRE HUSSARS

was quite unlike anything in his experience of a regular cavalry regiment. He was haunted by a fear that something must be wrong, and that there would be a breakdown when the strain of fighting was placed upon the structure. He wanted perfection, and he got it, but he did not realise it till he saw the Regiment in battle, for he failed to change the Yeoman outlook. But his outlook changed. He confessed as much after Bir el Gubi to an officer who was wounded early in the 1941 campaign. "After that," he said, "I understand a lot of things that were strange to me. No Regiment can touch them." He was a man of great humility and singleness of purpose. He had unlimited and unbounded pride in his Regiment and its achievements, and Gloucestershire Hussars will not forget him.

The Regiment formed up with 22nd Armoured Brigade a short distance north of Bir Bellefaa, and leaguered that evening by a block house in the same area. In addition to the Colonel and his crew, casualties were Sergeant Wilkins and Trooper Wallis killed and Lance-Sergeant Bayliss C. W., Troopers Lewis, Marks, and Porter wounded. The 7th was a quiet day, though eight tanks made a patrol to BIR EL RIGEL, and they were joined by the Brigade later. The leaguer that evening was south-west of Acroma, and we handed over our last two Grants. Lance-Corporal Harris and Troopers Bolt, Heard, and Nash were wounded.

The next day the Regiment became patrol squadron for the Brigade, and several reconnaissances were carried out with Major Trevor in command. A "Trevor Column" was proposed and the following morning it was further discussed. It was to consist of eighteen Honeys, six Crusaders, four Grants, one Squadron of armoured cars, one Troop of 25-pounders, one company of Infantry, and some 6-pounders, and it was to go through the minefield and harass enemy transport behind their line. The operation was to be known as "Arduous," but was quickly abandoned

THE LOSS OF MAJOR TREVOR

when news came of a German attack probably developing towards Knightsbridge. It was then decided to withdraw the Regiment to the Echelon near El Adem to refit, and to send H Squadron south of Bir Hacheim to join the 7th Motor Brigade. We reached the Echelon on their "minefield" on the 10th, and learned that Lance-Corporal Leaver, and Troopers Morris and Jones B. L., had been wounded by going over a mine the day before. On the 11th H Squadron moved off, and on the 12th the rest moved to El Mrassas, west of Tobruch.

This concluded the Regiment's battles as a Regiment. Henceforth we were to operate as one, two, or three Squadrons under commands other than our own. We had suffered grievous casualties during these sixteen days, seventeen killed, thirty-seven wounded, twenty-seven prisoners, and one missing, a total of eighty-two, and before we reached El Mrassas suffered one more, one that took away our remaining prop and mainstay. While waiting at the appointed rendezvous at Acroma to see the Brigadier, Major Trevor's car was dive bombed. He and Second-Lieutenants Boyd and Curgenven jumped out and threw themselves on the ground, but a bomb splinter struck Major Trevor in the back and killed him instantly. Bill Trevor had become Adjutant in April, 1940, and had nursed the Regiment through the difficult and aggravating months that preceded embarkation. He took over G Squadron just before we sailed, and commanded the Regiment from Sidi Rezegh till the end of 1941, and after the Colonel's death. He, like Colonel Birley, found Yeomanry ways somewhat strange, but his fears, too, were banished when the battle started. Campaigning under him made campaigning as pleasant as that difficult and dangerous task can be. He permitted himself no interference once his instructions had been given, and trusted everyone to carry them out unmolested. Even in the greatest heat of battle his orders on the air were quiet, audible, and completely intelligible. Above all, he inspired the Regiment with immense confidence, as he never asked it, or allowed it, to take on worse odds than he could help. The Regiment made its fighting name under him, and his loss was one from which it never recovered.

As well as those awards mentioned, Major Jerden received the M.B.E. He commanded the Echelon during this time with great determination and skill, and by his coolness rescued it on several occasions from shell fire and close proximity to the enemy. No refilling party ever failed to reach the fighting troops, and his example and spirit were an inspiration to his subordinate commanders. Regimental Quartermaster Sergeant Barnes, who had served the Regiment for 21 years, also received the M.B.E. for his part in keeping the Regiment fully supplied with spare parts, which were constantly needed, and never permitting a vehicle to be without what it required. This entailed tremendous work, and virtually no rest, and but for his tireless efforts the Regiment could not have gone on fighting as it did. Squadron Sergeant-major Hutson, for bringing his A.1 Echelon with untiring regularity to the tanks, though often under shell fire and on several occasions being forced to circumvent enemy columns, and for getting every vehicle to its destination in spite of difficulties which would have deterred a man of less determination, was awarded the M.M.

For three days we remained at El Mrassas. They were uneventful, though once some Italians had the impudence to dive in and bomb us, and the Germans did it at night, but no harm occurred. Major Lloyd and Major King spent the time visiting Brigade, Division, and Corps in attempts, which were successful, to prevent the Regiment being used for reinforcements and irrecoverably split up. The Germans were now approaching Tobruch, and furthermore were threatening to cut the road east of it, and so, being unhorsed and virtually unarmed, we were moved on

SIDI BISHR: JUNE 25th

the 14th to Salum. For four days we alternated between Salum and railhead at BIR MISHEIFA, the Higher Command not apparently knowing whether they, or we, were coming or going, and we were also told to join 8th Hussars and to provide one Squadron and an echelon to go with them on a harassing expedition. But this fell through, and on the 22nd we started eastwards, handing over our remaining vehicles to 4th County of London Yeomanry at FUKA, and, having staged at EL DABA, arrived, less H Squadron, at SIDI BISHR on June 25th.

* * *

H Squadron had moved off to join 7th Motor Brigade on June 11th. They reached Brigade H.Q. between Bir el Gubi and Bir Hacheim, and were sent on to join "July Column" which was, the Brigadier said, "operating somewhere between us and the enemy." He explained that the column's role was to harass the southern flank of the advancing Germans, and that a show of armour would help to put confidence into the hard-pressed French at Bir Hacheim. He added a cheerful confession that he knew nothing about tanks. But the French did, and withdrew from their positions the same day; it needed more than a Squadron of Honeys with 37-mm. guns to instil them with confidence at that moment. "July Column," besides H Squadron, consisted of a Battery and H.Q. from the Royal Horse Artillery, a company of the Rifle Brigade with a section of carriers, and a considerable number of 6-pounder anti-tank guns. It spent its time taking on enemy supply columns and unarmoured troops by day, and withdrawing south into the desert at night to leaguer. H Squadron's task was to protect the two gunner O.P.'s, and to destroy any transport that they could get at.

This continued for three weeks, a very tiring routine with a battle, generally a running battle, occurring on most days. The gunners always liked to shoot till the last possible moment, so that by the time a sufficient withdrawal had been made a "brew up" was frequently out of the question. A good day was experienced when one of the O.P.'s discovered a column of live transport hiding amongst some burnt-out vehicles south of the escarpment near El Adem. With the assistance of the carriers, two Troops and Squadron H.Q. sailed in and set on fire a number of enemy trucks. But the Germans got one back by knocking off Major Taylor's track with a 20-mm. anti-tank gun. The crew got to safety on a Rifle Brigade truck, and in the subsequent successful operations to rescue the tank Second-Lieutenant Stuart Jones was wounded in the knee and had to be evacuated. A short time later, on getting up at first light, it was discovered that a German column had leaguered during the night only four hundred yards away. Within a few minutes every gun was firing for all it was worth and, as the Squadron Leader's wireless was netted to Brigade for the moment, and there were three tanks on tow, the situation looked as if it might rapidly become critical. However, the enemy were even more discomfited, and scattered in every direction. A running fight ensued covering a large area of the desert, and order was restored with the help of other armoured formations who joined in as the battle passed them by. Towards the end, two unhappy days were spent with the Echelon bogged in soft sand, Brigade withdrawing, and the enemy advancing. But Captain Tubbs, who was commanding the Echelon, managed to extricate his vehicles and keep the tanks moving with supplies. By now crews were very tired and tanks were falling by the wayside, so on June 27th the Squadron handed over to a Squadron of the 8th Hussars, and lent them Second-Lieutenant Crawford and his troop. The remainder returned to Sidi Bishr, arriving there on the 28th. Casualties during this time were two killed, seven wounded, and one prisoner of war.

On June 28th G Squadron, under Major Lloyd, and with its Echelon, joined 1st Armoured Division Tank

THE ALEXANDRIA DEFENCE FORCE AT MEX

Delivery Regiment at EL HAMMAM, and on the 29th F and H Squadrons, under Major King, went as part of the Alexandria Defence Force to MEX, a suburb in the slums of Alexandria. There we were told to hold a canal running from the sea to LAKE MARYÛT, a distance of about half a mile. We were to act as infantry with Italian anti-tank rifles, hand grenades, and Molotov cocktails, and we discovered that we were in the last defended position in Alexandria. The remnants of Eighth Army were to go through, when some R.E.'s would blow up the road and rail bridges, and the R.G.H. were to fight the victorious Afrika Corps till they had nothing left, not even a cocktail. Nor was the fact that the line was still seventy miles away particularly comforting, since, if there was a break-through, it was only two hours' quiet motoring, and they would have been upon us. We remained there just under a week, bathing in the canal by day and being peppered by our own anti-aircraft splinters by night, for Alexandria was bombed regularly at that time. We fired the Italian Bredas into the lake to discover how they worked, estimated how far we could throw a hand grenade, but took no chances with the Molotov cocktails. And, with difficulty, we stomached the smells peculiar to that part of Alexandria. On July 4th the crisis was considered over, and we returned to R.H.Q. at Sidi Bishr.

G Squadron had set off to El Hammam on June 28th and joined 1st Armoured Division Tank Delivery Regiment that evening. The tank crews went up sandwiched in a ten-tonner with a trailer as the New Zealand Division, which was on its way to the front, was using all the available transport. After various vicissitudes they and their Honeys reached 22nd Armoured Brigade, who were just going into an attack near ALAM BAOSHAZA. All the available armour, and a motley collection it was, under 1st Armoured Division, were holding the south part of the middle of the El Alamein line, which was still in the process of being formed, and they were trying to prevent German infiltration by establishing a firm line in the best positions.

The Squadron joined in the attack on its arrival and then leaguered by Brigade H.Q. This was shelled in the morning by a Mk. IV that had crept up behind a ridge, and Second-Lieutenant Jaques was wounded in the leg, later having to have it amputated. The rest of the day was spent protecting Brigade H.Q. on one flank or the other, and at last light, when it was almost too dark to see, a Squadron attack was put in. On the following day they came under command of 4th County of London Yeomanry and attacked with them in the afternoon. A few prisoners were captured, but the order to return was given before much progress had been made. They were later shelled while sitting in the open behind R.H.Q., and Captain Milvain's tank received a direct hit, his driver, Trooper Pavey, being killed. That night, very late, they were ordered to hand over their Honeys in return for Crusaders, but as everyone was very tired, it was done early next morning, and a troop from 3rd County of London Yeomanry, a troop from 4th County of London Yeomanry, another of Valentines from the Tank Delivery Regiment, and the Brigade protective troop were added to the Squadron. While this was going on some Stukas paid a visit, and they were closely followed by Major-General Lumsden, who gave a stirring and encouraging address. Northing further occurred till the evening, when orders were received to join the 9th Lancers. They were by now a composite force, and during the Squadron's stay with them had, in addition to two Squadrons of their own and G Squadron, a 4th Hussar Squadron, a Bays, and a Greys Squadron. Three weeks were spent with the 9th Lancers holding one or other of two ridges south and east of the EL RUWEISAT ridge, getting into position half an hour before dawn and withdrawing half an hour after dark, patrolling and reporting, with shelling from time to time, three days up and one day back, maintaining and resting. The work

AT DAMANHUR AS CANAL GUARD

was very hard on wireless batteries, and though the Brigade Signals Officer produced many more than were permitted by the establishment, it was difficult to get them charged, and sometimes a tank in keeping its battery up would be out of petrol from stationary running and have to be towed into leaguer. Command alternated from 22nd Armoured Brigade to 2nd Armoured Brigade, and regiments and brigades differed almost daily as they came up from Tank Delivery Regiment or went back to refit.

After about a week with the 9th Lancers the Squadron knocked out and captured intact a Mk. II, which was foolish enough to put its nose over a nearby ridge, and this was shortly followed by an attack and an advance of five miles. During the battle Sergeant Gladman and Trooper Wright were killed, and Second-Lieutenant Boyd and Trooper Brett were wounded all by the same anti-tank gun at close range and in a few minutes. This advance established a position on a ridge looking into the Wadi DEIR ES SHEIN, but it was a German strong point, and no further progress could be made. The Squadron stayed in this locality for some time, and Second-Lieutenant Kirkby[1] was killed by a machine gun bullet while on patrol, and Second-Lieutenant Jeffery wounded when his tank was hit by an 88-mm. gun. On July 22nd, having handed over their tanks, the Squadron returned to Sidi Bishr.

During this time R.H.Q., F, and H Squadrons, under Major King, were sent to DAMANHUR as canal guard, since it was thought Rommel would attempt a parachute landing in that area. We moved there on July 5th and came under 10th Armoured Division. We were camped on a road inches deep in dust between two canals and a few hundred yards from a sewage farm. The smells were, at least, country smells, and better than those at MEX, but the heat

---

[1] Second-Lieutenant Kirkby had commanded the A.1 Echelon with great efficiency and calmness during the difficult period of May 27 to the end of the Knightsbridge battle.

was intense and sticky, and the mosquitoes were more numerous than can be imagined. At night, in the open, one forced one's way against them, and in a tent they swarmed in clouds and invaded mosquito nets in large numbers. Sores became numerous and serious, and it was here that the germ was caught that later resulted in several cases of diphtheria. After about a week tank crews, under Major Taylor, were ordered to KHATATBA to be ready to go up as reinforcements, but none were ever called for. They spent, however, a fortnight in great heat and glare, the monotony being sometimes relieved by a trip into Cairo. By July 22nd the whole Regiment was back at Sidi Bishr hoping to be reformed under Lieutenant-Colonel Cooper, who had just been posted to us.

On July 31st H Squadron were ordered to relieve A Squadron 5th Royal Tank Regiment, who came back for a rest and shared the Regiment's camp. Having taken over Crusaders at EL AMIRIYA they joined 5th Royal Tank Regiment in the middle of the El Alamein line at DEIR EL RAGIL. Lieutenant Meade was injured while loading the tanks on to transporters, but returned shortly. August was spent practising moving from leaguer to a number of defensive positions, so that virtually any attack by the enemy could be countered. Training was also carried out in the role of protective light squadron to an armoured regiment. During this time four crews of Americans were attached to the Squadron. They were to get operational experience, including seventy-six hours of fighting, and then to go back to the United States to train American armour in the Arizona Desert. Some training with Grants was also done, and by the end of August all tank commanders knew the desert they might have to fight over intimately.

On August 10th Major King went up to command C Squadron, 5th Royal Tank Regiment, and on the 17th F Squadron crews took over from them, and some more Americans were attached. On the 10th also, G Squadron

THE PRIME MINISTER INSPECTING R.G.H.

R.S.M. LEE

To face page 80

A PARACHUTE SCARE

had gone up to El Amiriya to take over Crusaders and remain as Army reserve. They started training and were, as well, at short notice in case of a parachute attack in the Alexandria area. On August 25th most of the Echelon and some of R.H.Q. under Captain Pitman were sent to KAFR EL ZAIYÂT to guard road and rail bridges as there was yet another parachute scare. They left at midnight, having had to wait for code words from Area until just after the moon had gone down, so that they had a thoroughly unpleasant journey with every chance of sweeping a farm wagon into one of the canals, if not going into it themselves. The country was such that the small arms carried were quite inappropriate to deal with the expected attack, but a happy-go-lucky staff officer proffered three 3·7 anti-aircraft guns. His suggestion was gratefully agreed to, as it was felt that the Regiment had had experience of so many weapons that something new, even a 16-in. naval gun, would not present insuperable difficulties. However, and perhaps fortunately for the neighbouring countryside, the scare passed before the guns were delivered, and the party returned to Sidi Bishr on the 28th. On the 29th Captain Pitman took F and H Squadron Echelons up to the line to relieve part of 5th Royal Tank Regiment Echelon, and the whole Regiment, apart from R.H.Q., was once more in position on the eve of battle, though not this time as its true self.

Meanwhile G Squadron had been re-equipped at El Amiriya with Crusaders and had done some training and practised shooting into the sea. During the training they took part in the first exercise ever done by Tactical Eighth Army H.Q. with a protective squadron, and they had the pleasure of leaving them with their vehicles, each commanded by an officer of Field rank, inextricably mixed up. During the numerous parachute scares the Squadron came under the 8th Hussars and then under an Indian Brigade with instructions to defend the Alexandria–Cairo road to the last ditch. But while the Brigadier was giving out his orders they were sent to 30th Corps H.Q., and were promptly passed on to 9th Australian Division, who had been in the line since it was formed and had withstood all attacks at Tell el Eisa and the El Alamein Box.

Here the Squadron formed the major part of a small column which was to create a diversion in the north if Rommel attacked round the south flank of the line. An Australian battalion was to punch a hole in the German defences west of Tell el Eisa allowing the column to pass through and do as much damage as it could in the direction of the SIDI ABD EL RAHMAN track. It was then, happy thought, to come back through the hole, its job done. This was not an attractive proposition, but after waiting ten days leaguering near El Alamein station, it was thought that the plan had been forgotten. But on the night of August 31st Rommel attacked and the code word BULIMBA was said. The Squadron moved forward to its concentration area west of Tell el Eisa station, and the Australians attacked. The hole was made, the signal to advance was given, and the Squadron moved forward in the early morning with beating hearts and the navigator's tank emitting clouds of steam. A delay now occurred, for the Australians, enthusiastically pursuing the Germans, had been counterattacked, and the gap had closed. Operation Bulimba, therefore, failed to materialize, and the Squadron returned to leaguer, to be sent off immediately to protect 30th Corps H.Q., and, with the 2nd South African Infantry Brigade, to form a defensive locality west of BIR EL THEMID. While engaged on this task, orders came to report to 10th Armoured Division, who were under 13th Corps, and from 10th Armoured Division the Squadron went to the 10th Hussars, who were so composite as to have three fighting squadrons, none of which was 10th Hussars. By now the general situation was well in hand, and the 10th Hussars and G Squadron remained static.

* * *

GENERAL MORSHEAD WITH G SQUADRON

TOBRUCH CEMETERY

To face page 82

LIEUTENANT-GENERAL MONTGOMERY

F and H Squadrons had settled down with B Squadron and R.H.Q. 5th Royal Tank Regiment and had done their reconnaissances and practised their battle drill until they were quite ready for the expected and now certain German attack. Rommel had been preparing for a long time, and was only waiting for the moon to be just right before launching his great and final offensive that was, his order of the day said, to take him to Alexandria and to Cairo, and thence north through Palestine to meet the German Armies driving south from Russia, and to close the giant pincers that had been threatening for so many months. He had as nearly as possible succeeded in July when Eighth Army, exhausted, beaten to their knees, and above all bewildered, had held him by the skin of their teeth. But there was to be no doubt this time. This was a carefully prepared set piece and success was sure, so sure that Mussolini ordered his white charger to be saddled. And the Afrika Corps had a surprise in store—the long barrelled 50-mm. and 75-mm. tank and anti-tank guns, the latter, at any rate, being nearly as good as the 88-mm. Against them, Eighth Army had the 6-pounder and many more of them and the 75-mm. tank gun, but nothing new, excepting Lieutenant-General Montgomery. But they had also, in the southern half of the line, perfect hull-down positions and alternative ones, and a flank resting on the QATTARA Depression that could not be turned. 22nd Armoured Brigade had, between them and the Depression, the 4th Armoured Brigade, 8th Armoured Brigade behind, and 44th Division on their right. Their orders were simple; fire to be opened at four hundred yards (for this purpose white posts were put out in front) and they were to fight to the last tank and the last round.

There was a code word for every position that might have to be taken up—pheasant and partridge, snipe, woodcock and 12 bore—suitable shooting words, though there was no mention of ground game or vermin, and considerable betting went on amongst the Americans as to which it

2ND ROYAL GLOUCESTERSHIRE HUSSARS

would be. At 2 o'clock on the morning of August 31st, "12 bore" was shouted into the ears of sleeping crews, and the Squadrons packed up and moved off to their appointed places while the A Echelons went back to B Echelon. By the middle of the morning it was evident that there were two strong columns of tanks that would interest 22nd Armoured Brigade, so H Squadron,[1] the light Squadron, were sent out to lure them on to F Squadron's guns. By 4 p.m. they were heavily engaged in front, and had three or four tanks brewed up from long range, but by withdrawing slowly they enabled F Squadron to open fire effectively. Then they came out to watch the left flank and wait in reserve. During the night six enemy tanks, endeavouring to find a way through, bumped into F Squadron's left flank and a sharp engagement took place between them and 2nd Lieutenant Summerell, who was the only person who could really see what was happening. One Mk. II was destroyed and the rest retired leaving the Squadron in peace for the rest of the short night. The battle continued, however, from dawn till the middle of the morning, and then from 5 in the evening till dusk. H Squadron, now with six tanks and assisted by some 6 pounders, stopped a flanking movement and turned the Germans on to a strong point, where they suffered considerable loss. They were then relieved by a Squadron of 3rd County of London Yeomanry and put in reserve, and whilst there came under heavy high explosive fire, and Lieutenant Turner was killed. F Squadron, hull-down, continued engaging anything within good range, and during the day had all twelve tanks hit and ten practically disabled, but managed to keep them fighting. Lieutenant Anderson and Sergeant Connor of the Americans and Trooper Burton were wounded,[2] Trooper Burton losing his arm. But the enemy were forced to retire.

[1] F and H Squadrons, as part of 5th Royal Tank Regiment, were commanded by Lieutenant-Colonel W. M. Hutton, D.S.O., M.C.

[2] Also wounded were Troopers Beer, Fletcher, Heard J., Oliver, and on Sept. 3 Trooper Leach.

LAST BATTLE AND GERMAN DEFEAT

The R.A.F. had been flying constant bombing sorties during the battle, and, on the night of September 1st, stepped up their activity, creating havoc in the enemy forming up and rear areas, so that in the morning when H Squadron went to look for the force of German tanks which had been visible the night before they found they had vanished. They had, however, kindly left behind a 150-mm. self-propelled gun, which was brought in—the first to be captured intact. The Squadron also knocked out two tanks and remained in contact all that day. By the morning of the 3rd the Germans had given up and were withdrawing quickly to their original positions. They had come up against good weapons and enough of them, good positions, and troops with the plan and determination to use them. In spite of their still superior fire power they had suffered very considerable losses and were back where they had started.

A few days later G Squadron rejoined and the Colonel and second in command, Major Little, who had recently come to us, visited the Squadrons and it was thought and hoped that R.H.Q. would come up and make the 2nd Royal Gloucestershire Hussars once more a complete Regiment in the battle line; but shortly after we received orders to return to Sidi Bishr.

So once again we climbed into our echelon lorries and set off, ploughing eastwards through the swirling desert dust.

* * *

Some time later it was learned that the battle[1] fought on August 31st to September 3rd, 1942, had brought to a close the Regiment's fighting career. During that career, which lasted just on one year, the 2nd R.G.H. suffered in casualties sixty-six killed, six died as a result of active service, one hundred wounded, and eighty-five prisoners of war. And it was awarded two D.S.O.'s, seven M.C.'s, one D.C.M., fourteen M.M.'s, two M.B.E.'s, and fourteen mentions in Dispatches.

[1] Battle of Alam el Halfa

Roll of Honour

O VALIANT Hearts, who to your glory came
 Through dust of conflict and through battle-flame;
Tranquil you lie, your knightly virtue proved,
Your memory hallowed in the Land you loved.

Killed

ADES, E., Lt.
ASTBURY, A., Tpr.

BIRLEY, N. A., Lt.-Col., D.S.O.
BUXTON, G. R., Tpr.
BYARD, A. H., Sgt.

CARPENTER, W., Tpr.
CHAMBERLAIN, J., L/Cpl.
CHARLTON, J. G., Tpr.
COLLIER, F., Tpr.
CONSTABLE, C., Sgt.
COOK, E. J., Tpr.

DAVIES, D., Tpr.
DOYLE, T., Tpr.

FRANCIS, D'ARCY, 2/Lt.
FROGGATT, W. G., Cpl.

GARDNER, F., Tpr.
GLADMAN, D. A., Sgt.
GLEDHILL, H. A., Tpr.
GODFREY, L., Tpr.

HAINES, E. W., Cpl.
HALL, W., Tpr.
HARNDEN, C. L., Tpr.
HARPER, J., Lt.
HASSALL, J., Tpr.
HELLINGS, S. R., Tpr.
HENDERSON, W. A., Tpr.
HILL, J., Tpr.

HONEYSETT, G., 2/Lt.
HOOPER, P., L/Cpl.
HOW, G., Tpr.
HUMPHRIES, V. A., Tpr.

JEFFES, C. E., Sgt., M.M.

KIRKBY, C. G., 2/Lt.

LANGSTON, P., Cpl.
LING, M. G., Capt., M.C.

MACKRELL, W., Tpr.
McREA, A., Tpr.
MITCHELL, A., 2/Lt.
MOSS, D., Tpr.
MUIR, H. M., Capt.

NOVELL, F., Tpr.

OVERBURY, L., Tpr.

PARRY, L., Tpr.
PAVEY, J. W., Tpr.
PLATT, J., Tpr.

REYNOLDS, R., Tpr.
REINHOLD, D. Mc.D., Major.
RIGDEN, F. G., Tpr.
ROBINSON, E. J., Tpr.
RUMSEY, E. T., Sgt.

SEABRIGHT, K., Sgt.
SERGEANT, C., Tpr.
SINNOTT, J., Major

ROLL OF HONOUR

South, C. E., Cpl.
Stephens, A., Tpr.

Trevor, W. A. B., Major, D.S.O.
Turner, R. I., Lt.

Wallis, P. N., Tpr.
Walters, P. A., Cpl.

Webb, D., Tpr.
White, G., Sgt.
Wilkins, K. J., Tpr.
Williams, W. N., Tpr.
Woodger, C. J., Sgt.
Wright, R., Tpr.

Young, M., Tpr.

Died as a result of Active Service

Fletcher, L. J., Tpr.

Hatton, L., Tpr.
Hollingsworth, J., Cpl.

Owen, K. N., Sgt.

Richards, H., Tpr.
Ward, E. L., Tpr.

Wounded

Ades, E., Lt.
Armstrong, F., Tpr.
Ayres, J., Tpr.

Barringham, F., Tpr.
Bayliss, C., Sgt.
Beer, A. R., Tpr.
Birley, N. A., Lt.-Col., D.S.O.
Bolt, N., Tpr.
Boughton, A., Tpr.
Boyd, G. G., 2/Lt.
Brett, F. D., Tpr.
Burton, B. S., Tpr.

Chew, N. G., Tpr.
Chiswell, J., Tpr.
Clark, H. V., Tpr.
Cook, T., Cpl.
Crane, W., Tpr.
Crowther, H., Tpr.
Cruise, J., Tpr.

Davison, L., Tpr.
Dickinson, L., Cpl.

Dimambro, A., Tpr.
Docherty, J., Tpr., M.M.
Donoghue, T., Tpr.

Edwards, H., Tpr.
Eighteen, G., L/Cpl.
Elder-Jones, T., Lt.
Elliott, J., Tpr.
Enoch, A., Cpl.

Fletcher, H., Tpr.

Gibbings, G., Sgt.
Gothard, W., Tpr.

Harris, A., Cpl.
Heard, J., Tpr.
Hill, W. R., Tpr.
Hosken, R., Tpr.
Hunt, S., Tpr.

James, T. G., Tpr.
Jaques, P., Lt.
Jeffrey, W. M., 2/Lt.

2ND ROYAL GLOUCESTERSHIRE HUSSARS

Jones, A. E., L/Cpl.
Jones, B. L., Tpr.
Jones, N., Tpr.
Jones, P., Tpr.
Jones, R., Cpl.
Jones, S., 2/Lt.

Kemp, H., Tpr.
Kermarec, P., Tpr.

Leach, J. W., Tpr.
Leaver, J., L/Cpl.
Lee, W., Tpr.
Leese, J., Tpr.
Lewis, J., Tpr. (twice)
Lockwood, C., Tpr.

Mallow, F., Tpr.
Marks, W., Tpr.
Marshall, A., Tpr.
Martin, H. G., Tpr.
Maynard, F., Tpr.
Mizon, H., Cpl.
Morgan, W., Tpr.
Morris, J. E., Tpr.
Morse, H., Tpr.
Mould, G. R., Sgt.
Murrow, F., Tpr.
Mylne, H., Major.

Nash, L., Tpr.

Ogden, A., Sgt., M.M.
Oliver, L. B., Tpr.
Oxborough, E., Tpr.

Pearce, P., Tpr.
Phillips, W., Tpr.
Ponting, N., Tpr.
Poole, W. A., Cpl., M.M.
Porter, R., Tpr.
Price, D., Cpl.
Proctor, J. R., 2/Lt.
Prosser, A., Tpr.

Reeves, E., Tpr. (twice)
Rich, T. F., Tpr., M.M.
Rowarth, J., Tpr. (twice)

Smith, K., Tpr.
Smyth, F., Tpr.
Summerell, A. J., 2/Lt., M.C.

Tomlins, W., Tpr.
Townsley, G. B., L/Cpl.

Watkinson, K. H., Tpr.
Welch, W., Sgt.
White, J. W., Tpr. (twice)
White, W. A., Capt.
Wiggall, A., Tpr.
Williams, G., 2/Lt.
Wilson, R., Tpr. (twice)
Winstone, R., Tpr.
Woods, E., Tpr.

P. O. W.

Adlard, R. E., Lt., M.C.
Amos, J. L., Tpr. (wounded)
Astley, T., Cpl.

Bates, C., Cpl.
Beard, H., Tpr.
Bell, W., Tpr. (wounded)
Booy, W., Tpr.
Bourne, E. J. S., Lt.
Bowers, T., Tpr.

Brewster, D., Tpr.
Bridle, V., Tpr. (wounded)
Brown, S. J., Tpr.
Burry, F., Tpr.

Carter, N., Tpr.
Chalkley, F., Tpr.
Clare, W., Tpr.
Clarke, A., Tpr.
Clark, S. W., Tpr.

ROLL OF HONOUR

CLAY, G. L., Lt.
COOK, T. C., Tpr.
CRADDOCK, D., Tpr.

DAVISON, G. F., Tpr.
DEAN, W., Tpr.

ELLIS, O., Tpr.

FURNIVALL, J., Tpr., M.M.
    (wounded)

GARDNER, D., Cpl.
GEORGE, S. T. (wounded)
GREAVES, K., Sgt.

HARMER, G., Cpl.
HARVEY, W. H., Tpr.
HAVINS, G., Sgt.
HEGGIE, A. J., Tpr.
HOUGHTON, C., Sgt.

JEWELL, F., Tpr.
JOHNSON, E. D., Tpr.
JONES, J., Tpr.

KNIGHT BRUCE, N., 2/Lt.
    (escaped)

LAPWORTH, W., Tpr.
    (wounded, recaptured)
LOVERIDGE, L., Tpr.

MALLON, P., Tpr.
MARKS, F., Tpr.
MARTIN, R., Tpr.
MERCHANT LOCKE, B., Tpr.
MORGAN, L., Tpr.

NUNN, R. G., L/Cpl.

OLIVER, F., L/Cpl.
OTTERBURN, A., Cpl.

PARRY, L., Tpr.
    (wounded, recaptured)
PARSONS, W., Tpr.

PATCHETT, L., Tpr. (died)
PATERSON, J., Capt.
PAVITT, F., L/Cpl.
PAYNE, G. W. (wounded)
PEARCE, P., Tpr.
PEARSON, J. V., Sgt.
PEEL, S., Lt. (wounded)
PIKE, S., Tpr.
PLAYNE, G. C., Capt.
    (killed while escaping)
POOL, A., Tpr.
PORTON, H., Tpr.
POSTLETHWAITE, T., Tpr.

RANDALL, M., L/Cpl.
READ, R. O., Tpr.
RODWAY, F. W., Cpl.
    (wounded)
ROGERS, N. H., Tpr.
RYALLS, H. R., Tpr.

SALEBY, J., Major.
SIMS, M. T., Tpr.
SIMS, R. M., Tpr.
SKINNER, J., 2/Lt.
SMITH, R. M., Tpr.
SNELL, H., Lt.
SOLOVITCH, C., Tpr.
STAGG, T. C., Tpr. (wounded)
STAITE, E., Tpr.

TIBBLES, F., Tpr.
TOVEY, H., Tpr. (died)

WADDELL, D. G., Tpr. (died)
WADLEY, L. J., Tpr.
WAKEFIELD, H., Tpr.
WEBBER, W., Tpr.
WIGLEY, F., 2/Lt.
WILKINS, R., Tpr. (wounded,
    died)
WOODS, N., Cpl.
WRIGHT, E., L/Cpl.

2ND ROYAL GLOUCESTERSHIRE HUSSARS

Awards

D.S.O.

BIRLEY, N. A., Lt.-Col.   TREVOR, W. A. B., Major

M.C.

ADLARD, R. E., Lt.   LING, M. G., Capt.
GORDON-CREED, G., 2/Lt.   MAUNSELL, R. E., Capt.
KING, N., Lt.   MILVAIN, E., Lt.
SUMMERELL, A. J., 2/Lt.

D.C.M.

YOOL, R., Cpl.

M.M.

A'BEAR, C. W., Sgt.   HUTSON, R. L., S.S.M.
ALLIES, D. G., Sgt.   HUXFORD, L. J., Tpr.
ANDERSON, A. V., Sgt.   JEFFES, C. E., Sgt.
BRACKENBURY, W. N., Sgt.   MORSE, H. N., Tpr.
DOCHERTY, J., Tpr.   OGDEN, A. R. G., Sgt.
DRAKE, R. D., Tpr.   POOLE, W. A. A. G., Cpl.
FURNIVALL, J., Tpr.   RICH, T. F., Tpr.

M.B.E.

BARNES, J. C., R.Q.M.S.   JERDEN, W., Major.

Mention in Dispatches

BALDWIN, F. K., Sgt.   MAUNSELL, R. E., Capt., M.C.
BIRLEY, N. A., Lt.-Col., D.S.O.   MUIR, H. M., 2/Lt.
BRACKENBURY, W. N., Sgt., M.M.   PALMER, F. S., S.S.M.
    PICKUP, M., S.Q.M.S.
ECKERSLEY, J. F., 2/Lt.   TREVOR, W. A. B., Major, D.S.O.
JEFFERY, W. M., 2/Lt.
LAWTON, T. H., 2/Lt.   VOWDEN, B. L., Cpl.
MARCHANT, B. C., S.Q.M.S.   WILLIAMS, G. C., 2/Lt.

INDEX

A Echelon, 84
A.1 Echelon, 23, 38–9, 64, 74, 79 n
A Squadron, 5th Royal Tank Regiment, 80
A'Bear, C. W., Sgt., 55
Acroma, 72, 73
Ades, E., Lt., 2, 29, 45, 57–61
Adlard, R. E., Lt., M.C., 25–8
Africa, North, 11
——, South, 1
—— Star, 10
Afrika Corps, 52, 56, 66, 77, 83
Agedabia, 42, 47
Alam Boashaza, 77
Alam Halfa, xix n
Alexandria, 1, 3, 47–8, 65, 77, 81, 83
Alexandria–Cairo road, 81
Alexandria Defence Force, 77
Americans, 80, 83–4
Amos, C., Tpr., 60
——, J. L., Tpr., 57–8, 60, 62
Anderson, Lt., 84
——, A. V., Sgt., 28
Antelat, 38n, 45
Apsley, Lord, D.S.O., M.C., 4, 45, 46 n
"Arduous," 72
Ariete Division, 10, 17
Arizona Desert, 80
Armoured Brigade, 1st, 49
—— ——, 2nd, xviii, 45, 52–3, 64, 79
—— ——, 4th, xviii, 8, 23–5, 33, 38, 46, 53–6, 64, 83
—— ——, 7th, xviii, 8, 23–5, 56, 64
—— ——, 8th, 83
—— ——, 22nd, xvii, xviii, 8–9, 23, 41–2, 48–9, 53, 67, 72, 77, 79, 83–4
Armoured Division, 1st, xviii, 1, 45, 52–3, 77
—— ——, 7th, xviii, 8–9, 32, 35, 53
—— ——, 10th, 79, 82
—— —— Tank Delivery Regiment, 76–9
Armstrong, F., Tpr., 16
Army Council Instructions, 6
—— Council, 6
Astbury, A., Tpr., 16

Astley, T., Cpl., 57
Auchinleck, General, 3
Australian Division, 9th, 82

B Echelon, 29, 35, 39 n, 64, 66, 84
B Squadron, 83
Baqqush, 48
Bari, 17
Barnes, J. C., R.Q.M.S., 30–1, 74
Bates, C., Cpl., 17
Bayliss, C. W., Lance-Sgt., 72
Bays Squadron, 78
Beard, H., Tpr., 13, 17
Beer, A. R., Tpr., 84 n
Bell, W., Tpr., 57–8, 60–1
Bellomo, General, 17
Bengasi, 16–17, 28, 38 n
Beni Yusef, 49
Besa guns, 3–5, 12, 20
Bir Bellefaa, 63, 66, 70, 72
—— Berraneb, 23
—— Duedar, 9, 11
—— el Aslagh, xix, 65, 67
—— el Gubi, x, 10–11, 29, 33–4, 47 54, 63, 72 ,75
—— el Harmat, x, 52, 58, 64 67, 69
—— el Rigel, 72
—— el Themid, 82
—— er Reghem, 23, 33
—— es Sufan, 49
—— Hacheim, 53–4, 58, 73, 75
—— Halegh el Eleba, 38
—— Misheifa, 75
—— Zeidam, 38
"Birley Force," 48
Birley (Charles), N. A., Lt-Col., xvii, 1, 11, 15–16, 47–8, 70–1, 73
"Bolo," 3
Bolt, N., Tpr., 72
Booy, W., Tpr., 37
Boughton, A., Tpr., 57
Bourne, E. J. S., Lt., 16, 27–9, 32
Bowers, T., Tpr., 28
Boyd, G. G., 2/Lt. (Regimental Navigator), x, 38, 44, 73, 79
"Box," 51, 53, 55–6, 63
Brackenbury, W. N., Sgt., 65

91

INDEX

Breda gun, 77
Brenchley, Capt. (Technical Adjutant), 29, 39
Brenner, the, 10
Brett, F. D., Tpr., 79
Brewster, D., Tpr., 44
Bridle, V., Tpr., x, 57–8
Brigade Echelon, 29
Bu Scihan, 10
Bulimba Operation, 82
Burry, F., Tpr., 57
Burton, B. S., Tpr., 84–5
Buxton, G. R., Tpr., 57, 59–60
Byard, A. H., Sgt., 57, 60–1
Byers, Sgt., 39 n
Bywater, Sgt., ix, xi, 55

C Squadron, 5th Royal Tank Regiment, 80
Cairo, 47, 49, 80, 83
Campbell, Brigadier, V.C., 35 n
Capuzzo, 49
Carr, Lt.-Col., xvii, xviii
Carsley, Sgt., 16
Carter, N., Tpr., 17
Caudle, Sgt., 28
Chalkley, F., Tpr., 28
Chamberlain, J., L/Cpl., 57–60
"Charlie," 3
Charles (Lt.-Col. Birley), 18
Chew, N. G., Tpr., 37
Chiswell, J., Tpr., 16
Chor el Ghisma, 44
—— es Sufan, 42
Chuer esc Sciah, 42
Clark, H. V., Tpr., 36
Clarke, A., Sgt., 17
Clay, G. L., Lt., 16
Clyde, 1
Collier, F., Tpr., 37
Composite Squadron, 65
Connor, Sgt., 84
Constable, C., Sgt., 37
Cook, E. J., Tpr., 16
——, T., Cpl., 63
——, T. C., Tpr., 63
Cookson, Lt., 27, 29
Cooper, Lt.-Col., 80
County of London Yeomanry, 18, 53
—— —— ——, 3rd, xvii, 9, 11, 14, 37, 42–3, 53–4, 56–7, 64–5, 69–70, 78, 84

County of London Yeomanry, 4th, xvii, 9, 11, 20, 27, 42, 53–4, 56, 67, 75, 78
Cowan, 2/Lt., 7
Craddock, D., Cpl., 17
Crane, W., Tpr., 70
Crawford, 2/Lt., 76
Crossman, 2/Lt., 12, 29, 38 n, 44
Cruiser tank, 61
Crusader tank, xviii, 2, 32, 49, 53, 57 n, 78, 80–1
Cull, Tpr., 31
Cunningham, General, 8
Curgenven, 2/Lt., 73
Currie, Lt.-Col., 35

Daba, 6
Damanhur, 79
"Dana," 3
Davies, D., Tpr., 15–16
Davison, L., Tpr., 57–8
Dean, W., Tpr., 63
Deir el Ragil, 80
Delta, the, 46–8, 51
Derna, 62
Dickinson, L., Cpl., 71
Dimambro, A., Tpr., 37
Docherty, J., Tpr., M.M., 71
"Double Blue," 36
Doyle, T., Tpr., 23
Drake, R. D., Tpr., M.M., 38

Echelon B., 29, 35, 39n, 64, 66, 84
——, Brigade, 29
Egypt, 1–2, 30
Eighth Army, xvii, xviii, xix, 5, 10, 16, 30, 52–3, 63, 66–7, 77, 83
—— ——, H.Q., 31
—— El Adem, 47–8, 63–4, 73, 76
—— Alamein, xix, 10, 67, 77, 80, 82
—— Box, 82
—— Amiriya, 1–2, 6, 80–1
—— Daba, 48, 75
—— Hammam, 77
—— Haseiat, 44
—— Mechili, 41–2
—— Mrassas, 46, 73–4
—— Ruweisat, 78
Ellis, O., Tpr., 28
Enoch, Cpl., 19–22

F Squadron, xix, 9–10, 12–4, 16, 29, 36–7, 40, 42, 44, 49–50, 51–2, 56–8, 62–3, 66–7, 69, 77, 79–81, 83–4

INDEX

Fiftieth Division, 53, 64
—— —— Box, 64
Fletcher, H., Tpr., 84 n
Fort Maddalena, 9
Forty-fourth Division, 83
France, xix
Francis, D'Arcy, 2/Lt., 45
Froggatt, W. C., Cpl., 71
Fuka, 75
Furnivall, J., Tpr., M.M., 15, 63

G SQUADRON, x, xix, 9, 11–14, 18, 35–6, 45, 49, 62, 64, 73, 76–8, 80–2, 85
Gabr Saleh, 23
Gagg, Tpr., 31
Garawla, 6
Gardner, D., Cpl., 28
Gatehouse, Brigadier, xviii, 38
Gazala, 35n, 48, 53–4
—— Box, 53
George, Tpr., 17
Germany, xix
Gezireh, 49
"Gippy Tummy," 4
Gladman, D. A., Sgt., 79
Gledhill, H. A., Tpr., 31
Gloucester, Duke of, 51
Gloucestershire Yeomanry, 1
Godfrey, L., Tpr., 69
Gordon-Creed, G., 2/Lt., M.C., 13, 21–2, 32–3, Capt., 51, 65
Gothard, W., Tpr., 65
Gott, Major-General, xviii
Grant tanks, xviii, 49–50, 54, 56–7, 66–7, 69–70, 72, 80
Greaves, K., Sergeant, 43, 57, 60–2
Greece, 29
Greys Squadron, 78
Griffiths, Cpl., 63
Guards' Box, 51, 53, 70
—— Brigade, 22nd, 38

H SQUADRON, x, xix, 9, 11–13, 18, 25–6, 35–8, 44, 49, 55, 62, 64, 66, 69, 73, 75, 77, 79–81, 83–5
Haines, E. W., Cpl., 37
Halfaya, x, 30–1, 47
Hall, W., Tpr., 65
Harmer, Cpl., 12, 37
Harnden, C. L., Tpr., 37
Harper, J., Lt., 12, 16

Harris, A., L/Cpl., 72
Hart, Capt., 27, 29
Harvey, W. H., Tpr., 57, 60
Hassall, Tpr., 45
Havins, G., Sgt., 17
Heard, J., Tpr., 72, 84
Heggie, A. J., Tpr., 28
Hellings, S. R., Tpr., 16
Hill, J., Tpr., 45
Honey tanks, xviii, 1, 32, 34, 66–7, 70, 72, 75, 77, 78
Honeysett, G., 2/Lt., 12, 16, 21
Hooper, P., L/Cpl., 45
Hoskin, Tpr., 37
How, G., Tpr., 43
House of Commons, 8
Houghton, C., Sgt., 63
Humphries, V. A., Tpr., 16
Hunt, S., Tpr., 65
Hussars (4th), xix, 66, 70
—— (7th), xviii, 5
—— (8th), xviii, xix, 35, 75–6, 81
—— (10th), 82
—— (11th), 9–11, 22, 24
Hutson, R. L., Sq. Sgt.-Major, M.M., 74
Hutton, W. M., Lt.-Col., D.S.O., M.C., 84 n
Huxford, L. J., Tpr., M.M., 34

IBBOTT, Lt., 39 n
Indian Brigade, 70, 81
—— Division, (4th), 35 n, 40
Indians, 67–8
Italian Ariete Division, 10
Italy, xix, 29

JAQUES, P., 2/Lt., 78
Jago, Lt.-Col., xvii
Jeffes, C. E., Sgt., M.M., 15, 33–4, 37
Jeffery, W. M., 2/Lt., 65, 79
Jerden, Lt., 7, 30–1
——, W., Major, M.B.E., 63, 74
Jewell, F., Tpr., 57
Johnson, E. D., Tpr., 17
Jones, A. E., L/Cpl., 30
——, B. L., Tpr., 73
——, Lt. Elder, xii, 12, 16–17
——, J., Tpr., 44
——, P., Tpr., 45
——, R., Cpl., 33
——, Stuart, 2/Lt., 76

INDEX

Jones, N., Tpr., 57
"July Column," 75

KAFR el Zaiyât, 81
Kemp, H., Tpr., 44
Kermarec, Tpr., 63
Khatatba, 80
King, Lt., M.C., 27–30, 40, 42, 44
——, Major, M.C., 57, 64, 69, 74, 77, 79–80
Kirkley, C. G., 2/Lt., 79
Knight, Major, 66
Knight-Bruce, 2/Lt., 53
Knightsbridge, x, 10, 35, 73, 79 n
—— Box, 62–3

LANCERS, 9th, 64, 78–9
Langston, P., Cpl., 45
Lapworth, W., Tpr., 17
Lawton, T. H., 2/Lt., 29, 39
Leach, J. W., Tpr., 84 n
Leatham, Colonel, 11
Leaver, J., L/Cpl., 73
Lee, Reg. Sgt.-Major, 65
——, Squadron Sgt.-Major, x, 30–1
——, J., Tpr., 19
——, W., Tpr., 16
Leese, J., Tpr., 44
Lewis, J., Tpr., 72
Libya, 9, 20
Libyan Sheferzen gap, 30
Light Aid Detachment, 39 n
Ling, M. G., Capt., M.C., 24, 27, 33–4, 45
Little, Major, 85
Llewellyn, Rev. W., xi
Lloyd, Capt., 8, 29–31
Lloyd, Capt., 8, 29–31, Lt-Col., D.S.O., x, xi
——, Major, 74, 76
L.O.B. Camp, 8
Lockwood, C., Tpr., 63
Looker, Cpl., 31
Loveridge, L., Tpr., 29
Lumsden, Major-Gen., xviii, 45, 52, 78
Luneberg Heath, 10

M.13 (Italian), 10–11, 13, 18–20, 22
Mackrell, W., Tpr., 63
McRae, A., Tpr., 16, 19–21
Maddalena, Fort, 9
—— Ridotta, 6

Mallon, P., Tpr., 28
Mallow, F., Tpr., 16
Mark IV (British), 23, 25, 32
—— II (German), 11, 32, 51, 79, 84
—— III (German), 11, 44, 49, 63, 66
—— IV (German), 11, 13, 49, 63, 66, 69, 78
Marks, W., Tpr., 44, 72
Marshall, A., Tpr., 63
Martin, H. G., Tpr., 44
Maryût, Lake, 77
Matilda tanks, 64
Maunsell, R. E., Capt., M.C., 69
Maynard, F., Tpr., 63
Meade, 2/Lt., 64, 80
Merchant-Locke, B., Tpr., 63
Merritt, Tpr., 31
Mersa Matruh, 6, 47
Messerschmitt, 35, 40
Mex, 77, 79
Middlesex Yeomanry, 39n
Miller, Jack, Lt.-Col., O.B.E., xvii
Milvain, E., Lt., M.C., 32–3, 46
——, Capt., M.C., 78
Minqar Miliha, 6
Mitchell, A., 2/Lt., 43
Mizon, H., Cpl., 69
Molotov cocktails, 77
Montgomery, Field-Marshal (then Lt.-Gen.), xvii, 10, 83
Morgan, L., Tpr., 13, 17
——, W., 16
Morris, J. E., Tpr., 73
Morse, H., Tpr., 46, 57
Moss, D., Tpr., 45
Motor Brigade, 7th, 53, 73, 75
Msus, 48
Muir, H. M., Capt. (Intelligence Officer), 7, 15, 27, 33, 35, Capt., 71
Murrow, F., Tpr., 16
Mussolini, 83
Mylne, H., Major, 5, 15, 18, 23, 25–6, 29, 35

N.A.A.F.I., 1
Naduret el Ghesceuasc, 52
Nash, L., Tpr., 70, 72
New Zealand Division, 35 n, 77
Norman, Major-Gen., xix
Norrie, Gen., Willoughby, xviii, 1, 48
Northumberland Fusiliers, 51
—— Hussars (Anti-tank Regiment), 38

INDEX

Novell, F., Tpr., 65
Nunn, R. G., L/Cpl., 28

OGDEN, A., Sgt., M.M., 65
Oliver, F., L/Cpl., 13, 17
——, L. B., Tpr., 84n
Otterburn, A., Cpl., 28
Oxborough, E., Tpr., 65
" Oxford Circus," 6

PADRE, the, 8, 15, 30, 39, 42
Palestine, 83
Panzer Division (15th), 40, 54
—— —— (21st), 40, 54
Parker, Tpr., 13
Parry, L., Tpr., 16, 57
Patchett, L., Tpr., 43
Paterson, J., Capt., 12, 17
Pavey, J. W., Tpr., 78
Pavitt, F., L/Cpl., 57, 60–1
Payne, G. W., Tpr., 17
Pearce, P., Tpr., 28, 57
Pearson, J. V., Sgt., 64
Peel, S., Lt., 62, 64, 70
Perry, Cpl., 19–21
Petra, Tpr., 30
Phillips, W., Tpr., 30–1, 44
" Piccadilly," 6
Pike, S., Tpr., 57
Pitman, Capt., 57, 81
—— Lt., 6, 16, 25–6, 29
Platt J., Tpr., 30
Playne, G. C., Capt., 17
Point, 172, 34
——, 181, 11
Ponting, N., Tpr., 45
Pool, A., Tpr., 37
Poole, W. A. A. G., Cpl., M.M., 36, 58
Porter, R., Tpr., 28, 72
Price, Tpr., 4
Prime Minister, 8
Proctor, J. R., 2/Lt., 55
Prosser, A., Tpr., 63
Pyramids, the, 48

QA'RET Azza, 6
—— Ghârif, 3, 4
Qattara depression, 83

R.G.H. SQUADRON (2nd), 25, 32, 38, 48, 52, 54
Randall, M., L/Cpl., 37
Rear 30th Corps, 30

Reeves, E., Tpr., 45, 64
Regimental Navigator (Boyd, G. G., 2/Lt.), 38, 44, 73, 79
Reinhold, Major, 11–12, 18, 19, 25–6, 29, 37, 38 n, 41
Reynolds, R., Tpr., 15–16
Rich, T. F., Tpr., M.M., 37
Ridotta Maddalena, 6
Rifle Brigade, 75–6
Rodway, F. W., Cpl., 57–8, 60, 62
Rogers, N. H., Tpr., 63
Rommel, x, xix, 48, 52, 54, 67, 79, 82–3
Roosevelt, President, 1
Rowarth, J., Tpr., 44, 70
Royal Air Force, 85
—— Armoured Corps, xix
—— Army Service Corps, 9
—— Engineers, 66, 77
—— Horse Artillery, 75
—— —— ——, (2nd), 38, 40
—— —— ——, (107th S. Notts Hussars), 51
—— Tank Regiment (2nd), 25–6, 32
—— —— —— (3rd), 38, 40
—— —— —— (5th), 28, 38, 40, 80–1, 83, 84 n
—— —— —— ——B Squadron, 83
—— —— —— —— C Squadron, 80
Rudge, Tpr., 30
Rumsey, E. T., Sgt., 43
Ryalls, H. R., Tpr., 64

SALEBY, J., Major, 13, 16
Salum, 8, 47, 75
—— Bay, 31
Saunnu, 41
Scott-Cockburn, Brigadier, xvii
Sergeant, C., Tpr., 57
Sheferzen, 30
Sicily, xix
Sidi Abd el Rahman, 82
—— Bishr, 2 n, 75–7, 79–81, 85
—— —— Camp, 48
—— Rezegh, 9–10, 23, 33, 73
—— Suleiman, 30
Sims, Tpr., 17, 28
Sinnott, J., Major (H.Q. Sq. Leader), 8, 29–30
Skinner, J., 2/Lt., 28
Slee, 2/Lt., 44, 69
Smail, Major (11th Hussars), 10

95

INDEX

Smith, K., Tpr., 16
——, R. M., Tpr., 28
Snell, H., Lt., 6, 9, 25–6, 28
Solovitch, C., Tpr., 57, 59–60
South Africans, 23–7, 53, 56
—— —— Infantry Brigade, 82
——, C. E., Cpl., 12, 16
Sphinx, the, 48
—— Bays, 78
—— Greys, 78
——, Composite, 64, 65, 66
Stagg, T. C., Tpr., 17
Staite, E., Tpr., 17
Stephens, A., Tpr., 45
Stukas, 36–7, 40, 43, 78
Strathmore, H.M.T., 1
Suez, Port, xviii, 1
Summerell, A.J., 2/Lt., M.C., 58, 64, 84
—— Sq. Sgt.-Major, 29, 30, 31
Support Group, H.Q., 35

TACTICAL Eighth Army H.Q., 81
Tank Reinforcement Squadron, 66
Tanks—
　Cruiser, xvii, 61
　Crusader, xvii, xviii, 2, 32, 49, 53, 57 n, 72, 78, 80–1
　Grant, xviii, 49–50, 54, 56–7, 66–7, 69–70, 72, 80
　Honey, xviii, 1, 32, 34, 66–7, 70, 72, 75, 77–8
　Mark IV (British), 23, 25, 32
　—— II (German), 11, 32, 51, 79, 84
　—— III (German), 11, 44, 49, 63, 66
　—— IV (German), 11, 13, 49, 63, 66, 69, 78
　Matilda, 64
　Valentine, 78
Taylor, Capt., 66
——, Major, x, 69, 70–1, 76, 80
Technical Adjutant (Brenchley, Capt.), 29, 39
Tell el Eisa, 82
Thirteenth Corps H.Q., 82
Thirtieth Corps, 7
—— —— H.Q., 82
Tibbles, F., Tpr., 28
Tmimi, 35n, 40
Tobruch, xix, 9–10, 32, 46, 48, 53, 63–4, 73–4

Tomlins, W., Tpr., 70
Tovey, H., Tpr., 57
Townsley, Tpr., 37
" Trevor Column," 72
Trevor, W. A. B., Major, D.S.O., x, 23–5, 32, 34–5, 37, 41–2, 72–3
Trigh Capuzzo, 32, 46
Tripoli, 7, 41
Tubbs, Capt., 76
Tuck, Tpr., 30
Turner, R. I., Lt., 84

VALENTINE tanks, 78
Vowden, Tpr., 15

WADDELL, Tpr., 17
Wadi Deir es Shein, 79
Wadley, Tpr., 17
Wakefield, Tpr., 17
Wallis, Tpr., 72
Walters, Cpl., 65
Warminster, 1
Waters, Capt. (M.O.), x, 4, 29, 39
Wavell, 10
Webb, Tpr., 58
Webber, Tpr., 17
White, Capt., 4, 6, 16
——, Major, 48, 66
——, Sgt., 35
——, J. W., Tpr., 16
Wiggall, Tpr., 16
Wigley, 2/Lt., 32
Wilkins, K. J., 62
——, R., Tpr., 57
——, Sgt., 72
Wilkinson, Tpr., 37
Wilks, Tpr., 57
Williams, D., Tpr., 60
——, G., 2/Lt., 33, 44
Wilson, R., Tpr., 16, 63
Winstone, R., Tpr., 15–16
Wood, Tpr., 30
Woodger, C. J., Sgt., 16, 21
Woods, E., Tpr., 31, 37, 57, 58
——, N., Cpl., 64
Wright, E., L/Cpl., 28
——, Tpr., 79

YOOL, R., Cpl., D.C.M., 58, 69
Young, M., Tpr., 28

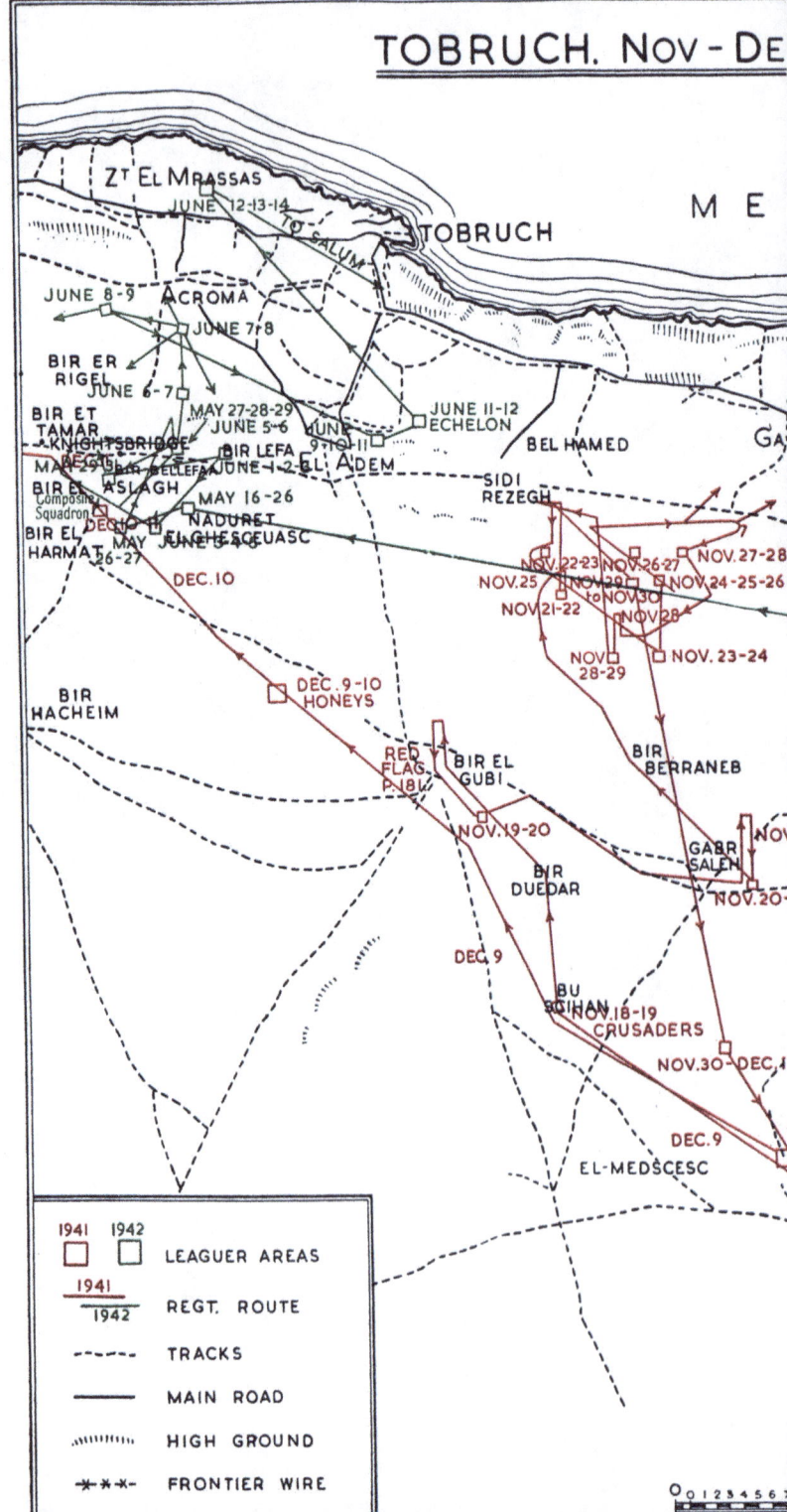

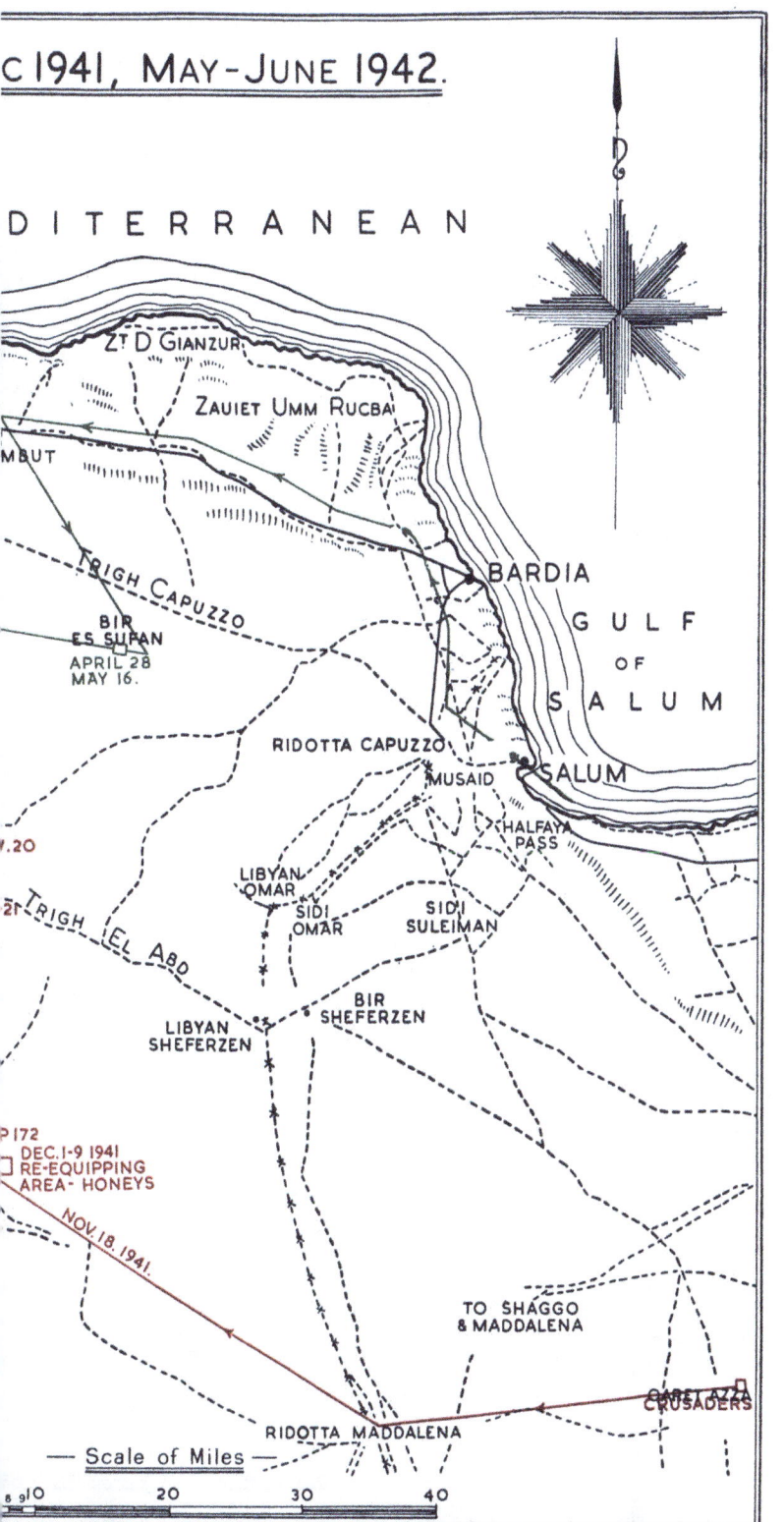

EL-MECHILI

EL-MECHILI

DAHAR EL-HALLAB

B. TENGEDER

DEC. 15-16
B-HAL
EL-EL

DEC. 18-19-20
21-22-23

DEC. 23

Legend

- ☐ LEAGUER AREA
- — ROUTE
- — MAIN ROAD
- --- TRACKS
- ᴧᴧᴧ HIGH GROUND

0 1 2 3 4 5 6 7 8 9 10

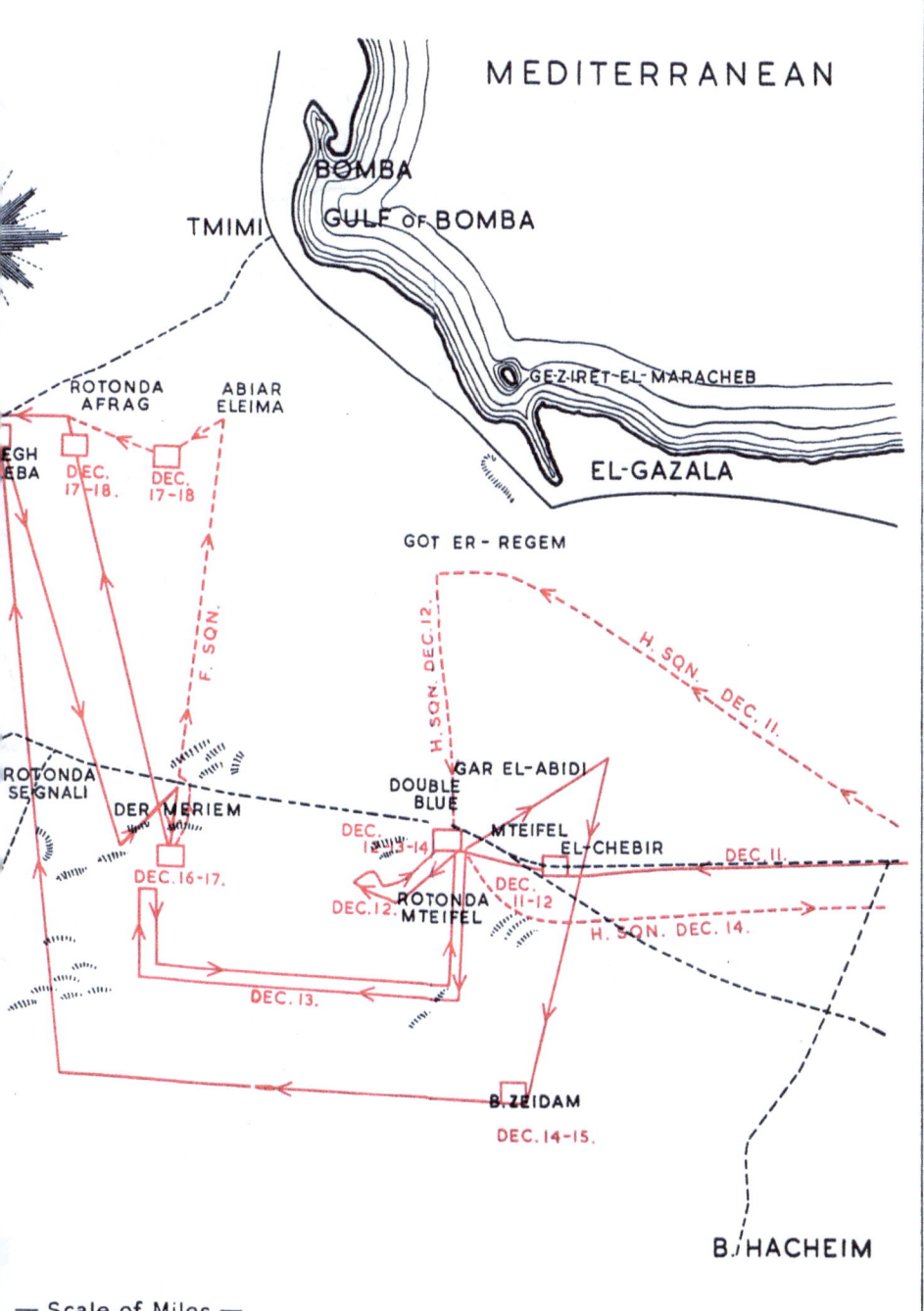

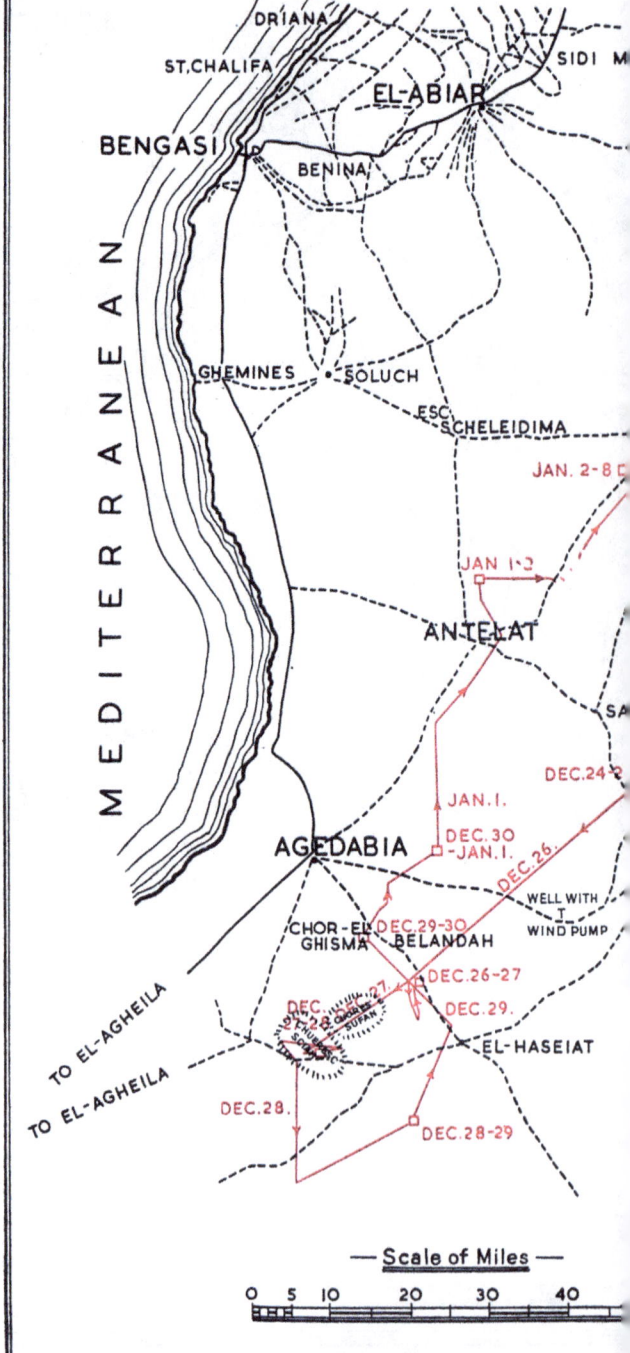

. 1941 - JAN. 1942.

AHIUS

ZT. MSUS

TO EL-MRASSAS

DEC. 23-24

DEC 24.

TRIGH EL ABD

UNNU

50

□ LEAGUER AREAS
— REGT. ROUTE
— MAIN ROAD
--- TRACKS
⌇⌇⌇ HIGH GROUND

EL-ALAMEIN. JU

- RAS-EL-DABA
- EL DABA
- M
- GHAZAL STATION
- SIDI ABD EL RAHMA
- TELL EL AQQAQIR
- TELL EL EISA
- DEIR E SHEIN
- EL MIREIR
- EL-KHARITA
- QATTARA DEPRESSION

Scale of Miles
0 1 2 3 4 5 6 7 8 9 10 20

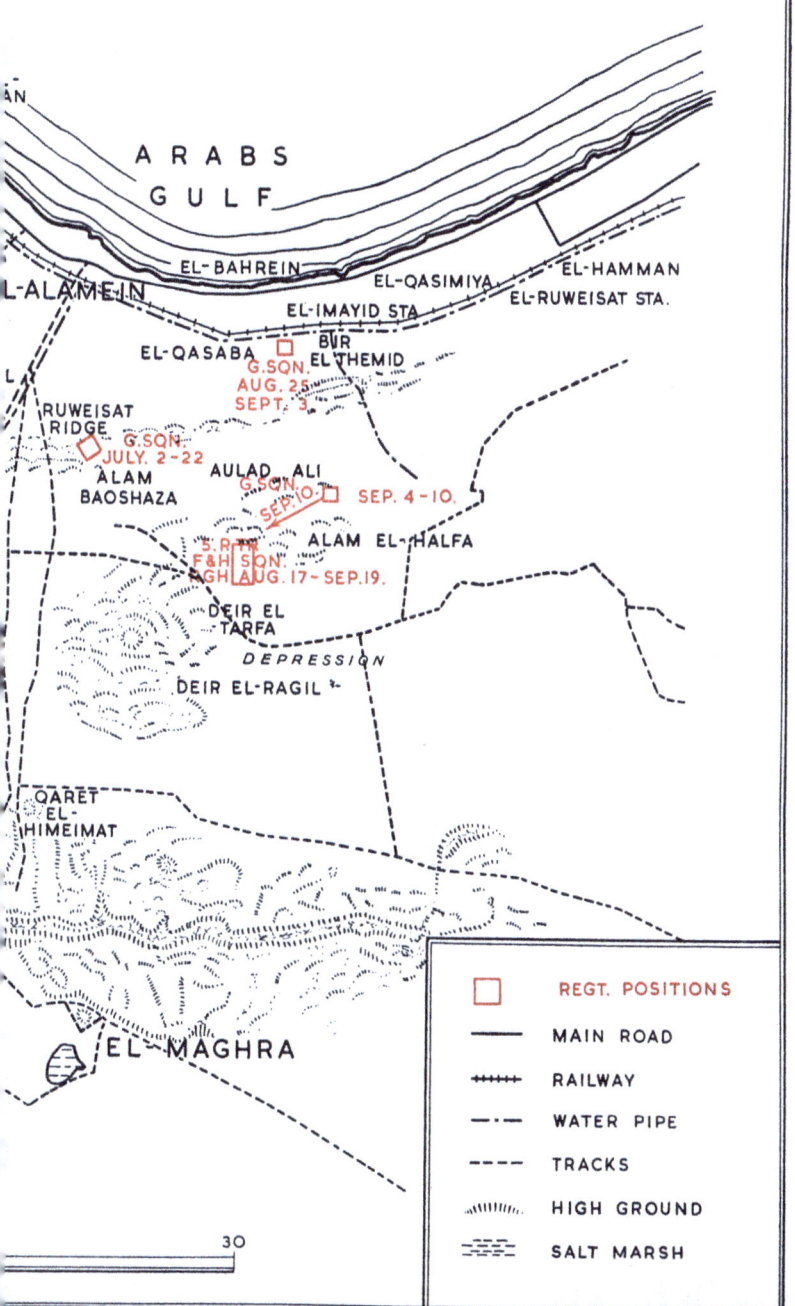

www.ingramcontent.com/pod-product-compliance
Lightning Source LLC
Chambersburg PA
CBHW060837190426
43197CB00040B/2660